Plants for

Pots & Patios

By

ROGER PHILLIPS
& MARTYN RIX

Research by Anne Thatcher
Design Gill Stokoe, Jill Bryan & Debby Curry

A Pan Original

Acknowledgements

We would like to thank the following gardens and
suppliers for allowing us to visit them and
photograph their plants:
The Royal Horticultural Society's Garden, Wisley;
the Royal Botanic Gardens, Kew; Cranbourne
Manor; Marwood Hill Garden; Levens Hall;
Kiftsgate Court; Powis Castle; Barnsley House;
Hestercombe; Eccleston Square Gardens; Chewton
Glen Hotel; the Harry P. Leu Gardens, Florida; Het
Loo; Denver Botanic Garden; Herrenhausen; Villa
Pallavicino; Villa Gamberaia; Hollington Nurseries;
Oldbury Fuchsia Nurseries; Read's Nursery.

Among others who have helped in one way or another
we would like to thank: Ann and Roger Bowden;
Sheila Bryan; Marilyn Inglis and Alison Rix.

First published 1998 by Pan
an imprint of Macmillan Publishers Limited
25 Eccleston Place, London SW1W 9NF
and Basingstoke
Associated companies throughout the world
ISBN 0-330-35547-3
Copyright in the text and illustrations
© Roger Phillips and Martyn Rix
The right of the authors to be identified as the
authors of this work has been asserted by them in
accordance with the Copyright, Designs and
Patents Act 1988.
All rights reserved.

9 8 7 6 5 4 3 2 1
A CIP catalogue record for this book is available
from the British Library

Colour Reproduction by Aylesbury Studios Ltd.
Printed by Butler and Tanner Ltd. Frome, Somerset

Contents

Don't hurry to throw away your old pot, even when too small for its tree

Introduction

This book is designed to provide inspiration for filling containers, window boxes, hanging baskets and built-in planters, and to suggest plants suitable for growing between paving stones and in cracks in patio walls. With a little planning and forethought, colour and interest can be provided throughout the year and we have illustrated a diverse range of flowers and foliage to suit every need.

The book is arranged roughly in flowering order, from spring to autumn, although we have kept groups of bulbs, shrubs, perennials and trees together. As a general rule, we have categorized the individual plants as either evergreen or deciduous, described the overall size of the plant, flowers and leaves, and given indications of hardiness. Common names are given in bold Roman print, Latin names in italics; synonyms, abbreviated to syn. (other names for the same plant) are given in brackets.

Containers

The key to successful container gardening is regular, generous feeding and the continual provision of ample water without letting the pots get waterlogged; in affect this means providing the largest, most generous container possible.

When preparing containers for planting it is important that they are clean and provided with sufficient drainage holes. To stop worms from coming up through the holes, and prevent waste of water, stand pots in saucers in summer and on top of saucers in winter or in very wet seasons. To prevent fine particles from being washed down and blocking the holes, put a layer of coarse stones or rough bark at the bottom of the container. Be careful not to use limestone chippings or rubble in pots containing acid-loving plants like rhododendrons, although these will be good for lime-loving plants like clematis.

As a general rule, plants that require more water do well in plastic pots, whereas drought-tolerant plants are happier in terracotta. New unglazed terracotta or earthenware pots must be soaked before potting to wet them and remove any salts.

It is possible to give new terracotta an aged appearance by encouraging algal growth. This can be done by painting the container with any medium containing nitrogen and keeping the surface damp; liquid manure or yogurt both work reasonably well. When planting a large chimney pot, keep in mind that only half the pot need be filled with compost, the rest can be filled with broken bricks or stones.

An annual review of containers will ensure that they look their best; shrubs and trees may benefit from being repotted, perennials divided, and both replanted into new soil. Feeding can be done either with liquid feed during watering, or by putting a measured amount of slow-release fertilizer onto the surface of the pot.

Positioning plants

Remember that the position of the container must suit the individual plants; some need sun whereas others prefer shade. Plants in containers have one great advantage over those in the ground; they can be moved to suit their requirements. Some, such as primroses, are best with sun in the cool times of year, but need shade in summer.

A fine show of petunias, begonias, bidens and hanging variegated ground ivy outside the King's Arms

Compost and care

Special compost for containers and hanging baskets is available from garden centres and this is suitable for most of the plants illustrated. Compost should crumble easily, retain moisture without becoming waterlogged, permitting free drainage and circulation of air, and contain the correct balance of nutrients and level of lime or acid; water-storing gel mixed into the compost before planting increases water retention.

Remember that plants do need attention if they are to be grown in containers for long periods and new compost will only provide enough nutrients for the first 6–8 weeks or so. Thereafter, many plants will need feeding weekly during the growing period, but less in winter or while dormant.

Trailing lobelias with *Helichrysum* 'Limelight'

Holidays

If you are unable to find anyone to water your containers while you are away, move them into a shady position; if it is summer, water them well and leave water in their saucers. Alternatively, place the entire receptacle into a loosely tied plastic bag; the bag above the tie will serve as a trap for any rainwater which will then trickle down onto the container.

Prunus glandulosa 'Rosea Plena' in the Forbidden City in China

5

Crocus vernus 'Striped Beauty' on the balcony at Eccleston Square

Spring Bulbs

In the chill of early spring, the cheerful colours of flowering bulbs signal a seasonal change of mood. Bulbs are ideal for containers, easily grown in sun or shade in a sheltered or exposed position and require little attention. The inevitably bare appearance of a bulb-filled container in winter can be avoided by planting the bulbs in small pots and transferring them when ready to flower; this method works well for some bulbs, but others are slow to establish and are better in more permanent plantings. Often the bulbs can be purchased just as they come into bloom, but these are likely to have been forced and will need a very sheltered position outdoors.

Needless to say, permanent plantings require less work after the initial effort and with a little thought can provide garden interest throughout the year. Bulbs planted in layers under perennials and shrubs remain undisturbed until they flower in spring; beware of mixing too many different types though, as this can result in a rather hotchpotch effect. It is often best to combine only a few varieties, or even restrict the selection to different colours or varieties of one type.

Dwarf bulbs are ideal for window boxes as they are less susceptible to wind damage, but taller varieties can look sensational grouped together in containers or planters. Bulbs can be removed and discarded after flowering, planted in the open garden or kept for another year in the pot. If they are to be kept, the leaves should be allowed to develop fully and watering continued until the leaves die down.

Greek Anemone

Anemone blanda   A dwarf that grows to 3in (8cm) high, producing blue flowers, about 1¼in (3cm) across, in March and April, flourishing in sun or light shade, dormant in summer. Hardy to −20°F (−29°C), US zones 5–9. Native to the E Mediterranean region and W Asia.

PLANTING HELP   Best planted in late summer or early autumn in any reasonable compost, 4in (10cm) apart, to a depth of 2in (5cm). The thick roots may be left in the soil for 3–5 years before lifting, dividing and replanting. To propagate, separate rhizomes in late spring or after the leaves have died down.

Mixed colours of *Crocus vernus*

Ipheion uniflorum 'Rolf Fiedler'

Crocus

Crocus vernus A bulb that grows 4–5in (10–12cm) high, with single white, purple or violet flowers, 1¼–2½in (3–6cm) long, from early spring to early summer. There are many cultivars with differing flower characteristics, including some with striped flowers. Hardy to −30°F (−35°C), US zones 4–10. Native to central and eastern Europe.

PLANTING HELP Plant bulbs in September, if possible, to a depth of at least 1½ times the size of the bulb. Prefers full sun. Divide clumps, if necessary, during the dormant period and propagate by removing offsets. Water and apply liquid feed every few weeks during the growth period; keep drier when dormant.

Spring Starflower

Ipheion uniflorum Native to rocky sites in South America, this bulb grows 6–8in (15–20cm) high with garlic-scented leaves in late autumn and single, star-shaped, sweet-scented flowers 1½in (4cm) across in late spring. The wild bulb produces pale blue flowers but there is a wider

Anemone blanda at the edge of a gravel path

choice among the various cultivars. Hardy to −10°F (−23°C), US zones 6–9.

PLANTING HELP Plant in any reasonable bulb mix in September, to a depth of at least 1½ times the size of the bulb. Prefers full sun. Divide clumps, if necessary, during the dormant period and propagate by removing offsets. Water and apply liquid feed every few weeks during the growth period; keep drier when dormant.

Hyacinths in a range of colours and containers

Grape Hyacinth

Prepared blue hyacinths grown in wet gravel

Hyacinths

Hyacinthus orientalis Native to the eastern Mediterranean region and North Africa, hyacinths have been cultivated for their dense spikes of scented flowers since the 16th century. They make excellent container plants. The individual flowers, ¾–1½in (2–4cm) long, pale blue in the wild, are borne in magnificent clusters; colours of cultivars range from white, yellow, pink and blue to deep purple and almost black, on stems 8–12in (20–30cm) high. The heady scent is irresistible so make sure they are put where this can be fully enjoyed! Hardy to 10°F (–12°C), US zones 8–10.

PLANTING HELP Plant bulbs 4in (10cm) deep and at least 3in (8cm) apart in autumn in any reasonable bulb mix. For sun or partial shade. Do not allow containers to become too wet in winter. Propagate by removing offsets when dormant.

Grape Hyacinth

Muscari armeniacum A bulb that grows to 10in (25cm) high, producing packed clusters of scented, soft blue, grape-like flowers on leafless stems in spring, and green leaves to about 12in (30cm) long in autumn. ***Muscari botryoides*** **'Album'** has white flowers. Wonderful for mixing with other bulbs. Both are hardy to –30°F (–35°C), US zones 4–8.

PLANTING HELP Plant bulbs 4in (10cm) deep in any reasonable potting mix in full sun. To maintain vigorous growth, divide clumps during

Paper Whites *Narcissus papyraceus*

Muscari botryoides 'Album'   *Narcissus* 'Jumblie'

summer when bulbs are dormant. Propagate by removing offsets in summer.

Daffodils & Narcissi

There are many different shapes and sizes of *Narcissus*, with flowers borne singly or in clusters in combinations of yellows, oranges and whites. They all make excellent container plants.

PLANTING HELP   Plant to a depth of 4–6in (10–15cm) in early autumn and water during growing period. To ensure the bulbs reach their full flowering potential in the second year, allow the leaves to soak up as much sunlight as possible, not cutting them back until they turn brown.

Narcissus papyraceus (syn. *N.* 'Paper White') Grows to 14in (35cm) high and produces clusters of fragrant white flowers ½in (1.5cm) wide, from winter to early spring. Hardy to 20°F (–6°C), US zones 9–10.

Narcissus 'Soleil d'Or'

Narcissus 'Jumblie'   Produces up to 3 two-tone yellow, pendant flowers 1¼in (3cm) wide, on each stem, 7in (18cm) high, in early spring. Hardy to 0°F (–18°C), US zones 7–10.

Narcissus 'Soleil d'Or'   Grows to 15in (40cm) high and produces clusters of sweetly scented, deep yellow flowers with orange centres, 1¾in (4.5cm) wide, in early spring. Hardy to 20°F (–6°C), US zones 9–10.

Narcissus 'Tête à Tête'   A good dwarf variety for the edge of a path, with stems to 7in (18cm) high and flowers in twos or threes.

Narcissus 'Tête à Tête'

Tulipa fosteriana 'Purissima' with a Cretan pot

Tulipa fosteriana 'Garden Party'

Tulipa kaufmanniana 'Heart's Delight'

Tulips

There are around 100 different wild species of *Tulipa* native to hot, dry regions from Greece and Turkey to central Asia. The greatest variety is found in the mountains of central Asia, but most garden tulips are cultivars and their history is dramatic.

In the 16th century, unusual shades or shapes attracted big money and in Holland in the mid-1630s a combination of exorbitant prices and obsession resulted in speculation in which thousands of people lost their life-savings. Even in the early 19th century, bulbs of 'broken' tulips (those with mixed, flamed or feathered colouring), commanded up to £150 each! The fact that these patterns are the result of infection by an aphid-transmitted virus was not suspected nor proved until the 20th century. These 'broken' tulips are still loved by gardeners and are sold as 'Rembrandt' tulips.

Fortunately, packs of tulip bulbs can now be

TULIPS

Lily-flowered tulip 'Aladdin'

Parrot tulip 'Estella Rijnveld'

Single early tulip 'Apeldoorn'

purchased quite cheaply, and autumn planting will ensure a superb show in late spring and early summer if varieties are chosen with a succession of flowering times. With their sturdy stems and large flowers in brilliant colours, the shorter-growing tulips are especially useful in smaller pots and window boxes, while the taller varieties look graceful and elegant in larger planters. Those illustrated represent only a selection of tulips, all of which make excellent container plants.

PLANTING HELP   Plant tulip bulbs at least 6in (15cm) below the surface, in late autumn or early winter in sun or partial shade; they look best in groups of four or more. Make sure the drainage is very good. The bulbs can be lifted after flowering and planted in a less conspicuous position among perennials to allow the foliage to die back slowly. Alternatively, store in pots laid on their sides in the shade after the leaves have turned yellow until autumn. In our experience, the size of the blooms is reduced in subsequent seasons, so if you want large blooms, buy new bulbs every year. Do not allow the soil to become dry between planting and the end of flowering, but avoid over-wet soil. Hardy to 10°F (−12°C), US zones 8–10.

Tulipa greigii 'Red Riding Hood' with *Narcissus* 'Golden Ducat'

Sweet Violets *Viola odorata*

Cultivated *Viola tricolor*

Wild Pansy or Heartsease

Viola tricolor   An annual or biennial that grows to 6in (15cm) tall bearing violet, yellow or bicoloured flowers, 1in (2.5cm) across, throughout the summer. Leaves heart-shaped to 1¼in (3cm) long. Native to Europe, including Britain, especially in the north, and northern Asia. Hardy to –30°F (–35°C), US zones 4–8.

Sweet Violet

Viola odorata   An evergreen perennial that grows to 4in (10cm) tall, with heart-shaped, bright green leaves and fragrant purplish blue or white flowers ¾in (2cm) wide, in late winter into spring. Native to Europe, including Britain, but widely naturalized in North America. Hardy to 10°F (–12°C), US zones 8–10.

Cultivated Pansies & Violas

Small-flowered perennial violas that grow 4–12in (10–30cm) high, are perfect for planting between paving stones and gravelled areas as well as looking wonderful in pots and window boxes. While violas cannot be subjected to heavy foot traffic, they look exquisite when planted in a hidden path or between edging stones. However, planting in this way does require some work; trim plants hard in midsummer and propagate using young lower shoots. Hardy to 10°F (–12°C), US zones 8–10.

Pansies that grow 5–12in (12–30cm) high, are short-lived perennials which are usually grown as annuals or biennials. They are the very best of container plants, recognized by their large flat faces, often of many colours. We planted three terracotta pots full of mixed colours in March and they have rewarded us with a wonderful display; as we write this in late July, they are still looking sensational, showing no sign of going over. Indeed, great advances in breeding in recent years, particularly with winter-flowering varieties, mean that pansies can maintain a presence in the garden throughout the year, provided that the weather is neither too hot and dry, nor too cold.

The compact plants of the Fanfare series, which produce medium-sized flowers in a wide range of colours during winter and spring, are particularly good for hanging baskets. Hardy to 10°F (–12°C), US zones 8–10.

PLANTING HELP   For sun or partial shade. Pansies and violas are cheap and readily available from garden centres, although they can be easily propagated from seeds or cuttings. Plant in the latter part of March to ensure a good display in spring, or in September for a winter display. Pansies dislike too much rain but this should not be a problem if containers are well drained. Remove dead flower heads to lengthen flowering time and cut off old shoots to keep the plants compact. Snails and slugs hide under the stems of old plants and eat the lower leaves and flowers.

Pansy

Spring-flowering pansies in pots

A mixed planting of pansies in an urn

Spring pansies with *Cerastium tomentosum*

VIOLAS & PANSIES

Violas with lavender 'Papillon' in an urn with ivy

'Thompson & Morgan's Black Pansy'

Viola cornuta 'Boughton Blue'

A fine pot of blue pansies 'Velour Blue'

Pansy 'Imperial Silver Princess'

Pansies with *Crocus vernus* leaves at Wisley

Pansies and petunias in a hanging basket

Pansy 'Pink Panther' with *Iris kaempferi* flowers

Tulips, wallflowers and polyanthus in a grand setting

Aubrieta 'Lilac Cascade'

Alyssum *Aurinia saxatilis* and *aubrieta* on a wall in Wilton, Wiltshire

Spring Perennials

Perennials can be divided into herbaceous plants, which die back to ground level each autumn or winter, and those which are evergreen, keeping their foliage throughout the year. Many do well in containers, but are often neglected in favour of annuals. With very little effort perennials will appear faithfully year after year and with careful selection and combination they can provide flower or foliage interest for most of the year, mixing well with shrubs, trees and annuals.

Celandines and moss between paving slabs

Alyssum

Aurinia saxatilis (syn. *Alyssum saxatile*)
A plant that grows to 9in (23cm) high, producing low clumps of hairy greyish leaves, with clusters of yellow flowers in late spring. Native to C and SE Europe. Hardy to −40°F (−40°C), US zones 3–8.

PLANTING HELP   For full sun in any reasonable, well-drained compost. Propagate by seed sown in autumn or softwood cuttings in early summer.

Aubrieta

This mat-forming plant grows to 2in (5cm) high, bearing small greyish leaves and clusters of lilac flowers in spring. *Aubretia* does well in stone troughs or along the edge of paving stones. There are many cultivars in shades of red and mauve to bluish. 'Lilac Cascade' is one of the best. Hardy to 10°F (−12°C), US zones 8–10.

PLANTING HELP   Grow in full sun in any reasonable, possibly slightly alkaline potting compost and cut back after flowering to keep the plant compact. Can be propagated by seed sown in autumn or spring, although cultivars do not usually grow true to type.

Buttercups

Turban Buttercup *Ranunculus asiaticus*   Grows to 15in (40cm) high, producing single, double or semi-double flowers in red, pink, purple, yellow and white, 2½in (6cm) wide. Native to the Mediterranean region and W Asia. Hardy to 20°F (−6°C), US zones 9–10.

PLANTING HELP   Plant in autumn in frost-free areas or in early spring in any reasonable potting mix about 2in (5cm) deep in a sunny position. Keep moist but not wet. Dry completely after flowering.

Lesser Celandine *Ranunculus ficaria*   Grows to 2in (5cm) high, producing golden yellow to white flowers ¾–1¼in (2–3cm) wide, fading to white as they age. Double-flowered forms are pretty and many have marbled leaves. In mild climates these plants can flower from as early as December. Native to Europe, N Africa and SW Asia. Hardy to −20°F (−29°C), US zones 5–9.

PLANTING HELP   Plant in any reasonable potting mix in full sun. Keep moist during the growing season, but drier when dormant.

Wallflower

Erysimum cheiri (syn. *Cheiranthus cheiri*)
Grows to 2ft (60cm) tall bearing uniquely scented flowers in a wide range of colours in late spring and early summer. These plants like chalk and are particularly good for putting into cracks between paving stones and growing in stone troughs. The plants are more likely to prove perennial when growing between bricks or stones. In May, put a few seeds or seedlings in the cracks, with the addition of a little soil and well-rotted manure. Alternatively, young plants can be put out in autumn and thrown away after flowering. Wallflowers make an attractive addition to containers and the dwarf forms are ideal for window boxes and hanging baskets. Hardy to 0°F (−18°C), US zones 7–10.

PLANTING HELP   For well-drained, chalky compost in full sun. Propagate from seed planted in May or take softwood cuttings of the shrubby kinds in summer.

Turban Buttercup *Ranunculus asiaticus*

Wallflowers self-sown on an old wall

Lord Anson's Blue Pea *Lathyrus nervosus*, in a pair of large pots at Sissinghurst Castle, Kent

Prepared rhizomes of lily-of-the-valley in a shallow pan

Mixed polyanthus in spring

Lathyrus

Lathyrus nervosus Lord Anson's Blue Pea
A climber that grows to 5ft (1.5m) tall, bearing greyish green, leathery leaves about 1½in (4cm) long, and producing clusters of scented purple blue flowers on long stalks in early summer. Wonderful for growing through shrubs or up a trellis or hanging down in a tall pot. It may not survive outside in colder winters. Native to South America. Hardy to 20°F (–6°C), US zones 9–10.

PLANTING HELP   Plant in humus-rich potting mix in full sun or dappled shade. Feed every few weeks during growing season and dead-head regularly. Sow pre-soaked seed in containers in early spring.

Lily-of-the-valley

Convallaria majalis   Grows to 8in (20cm) tall, producing pairs of elegant leaves 1½–8in (4–20cm) long, and arching clusters of strongly scented, bell-shaped white flowers ¼–½in (0.5–1.5cm) wide, in late spring. Plant prepared rhizomes in a container to bring into the house when flowering, or put in a shady window box where the scent can be truly appreciated. Hardy to

–20°F (–29°C), US zones 5–10. Native to Europe and North America.

PLANTING HELP   Plant in rich, moist compost in shade by making a shallow depression, then carefully spread out the roots and pile loose leaf mould on top to cover completely. Top dress with leaf mould in autumn. Sow seed when ripe. Separate rhizomes in autumn.

Primula

The most suitable garden primroses for growing in containers are the Primrose-Polyanthus group, which flower during winter and early spring. Ranging from 3–6in (8–15cm) tall, they are now available in a wide range of colours and are ideal for window boxes and containers. Some have a single flower to a stem, like wild primroses; others have tall stems with multiple flowers on each stem, like the Cowslip parent. Hardy to 10°F (–12°C), US zones 8–10 or lower.

PLANTING HELP   Some shade will prolong the life of the flowers but most will tolerate full sun in spring provided their roots are kept moist. Keep plants shady and well watered in summer, especially in over-full containers.

Polyanthus around a fountain in a London square

Camellia 'Akashigata'

Camellias

Camellias lend an exotic touch to the garden from winter to late spring. Their attractive evergreen leaves provide a perfect foil for the thick-petalled flowers, and for annuals and bulbs during the summer. Be selective when choosing the variety of camellia to plant in a container. Dark, glossy green leaves look better than smaller, paler ones, and it is a good idea to choose a plant with a dense, compact habit rather than one which forms a straggly, untidy plant. Those camellias illustrated are only a selection from the many hundreds of forms and colours that can be grown in pots.

Camellias should be sheltered from cold winds and the early morning sun, and are happiest in areas of light shade under mature trees. They tolerate occasional drops to freezing, but it is wise to move plants into a cool greenhouse in winter if the area consistently experiences frozen ground and heavy snow; buds and flowers are damaged by icy winds and late frosts. Hardy to 10°F (−12°C), US zones 8–10.

Camellia × williamsii 'Debbie' in Eccleston Square

PLANTING HELP   Plant singly in autumn in ericaceous compost; the top of the root ball should be level with the surface of the soil. Little pruning is needed, although young plants can be lightly trimmed during flowering, and the previous year's stems can be cut back by between a half and a third to retain the shape of the plant. Propagate by means of semi-ripe cuttings in autumn, or leaf-bud cuttings in spring. Water regularly but infrequently; more when in flower, sparingly in winter. Camellias prefer partial shade. The ideal container size for a young plant is 8–18in (20–45cm). Repot every third year.

Camellia × williamsii **'Jury's Yellow'**   The only yellow-flowering camellia that is easy to find. It has dense, upright growth and will reach about 3ft (90cm) in five years.

Camellia × williamsii **'Donation'**   Produces masses of flowers and is fairly slow-growing, reaching about 4ft (1.2m) in five years.

Camellia **'Akashigata'** (syn. 'Lady Clare') Has a weeping habit, growing to about 3ft (90cm) tall and 4ft (1.2m) wide in five years.

Camellia × williamsii **'Debbie'**   Produces exciting double flowers, dense upright growth and will reach about 3ft (90cm) in five years.

Camellia **'Lavinia Maggi'**   A strong-growing camellia with striped pink and white flowers, reaching as much as 4ft (1.2m) after five years.

Camellia 'Lavinia Maggi'

Ceanothus

These evergreen or deciduous shrubs from the
Pacific Coast of the US produce abundant clusters
of tiny blue, white or pink flowers in spring or
summer, hence the name California lilac. The
smaller varieties are much the best for pots, since
the many other, more upright forms, such as
Ceanothus arboreus, are too large. **Ceanothus
'Blue Mound'** may grow to as much as 4ft (1.2m)
high and wide after five years; and
Ceanothus **'Snowball'** is
prostrate and very slow-growing,
reaching about 2ft (60cm) in
five years. These varieties are
hardy to 10°F (−12°C),
US zones 8–10.

PLANTING HELP
Prefer full sun and
shelter from cold
winds. They
are very
drought-
tolerent, so only
water in the first
year after planting.

Ceanothus
'Blue
Mound'

Ceanothus 'Snowball' hanging from a tall pot

Camellia × *williamsii* 'Donation'

Camellia × *williamsii* 'Jury's Yellow'

Rhododendrons & Azaleas

Rhododendrons and their hybrids make ideal pot plants, with attractive green foliage all year round and a short burst of flowers in spring. Most evergreen rhododendrons and azaleas are suitable for growing in containers; there are many hundreds of different forms in a great variety of flower colours and we have illustrated a few that we know to be successful. The deciduous azaleas exhibit spectacular autumn colour and their flowers are usually sweetly scented. The tender, scented rhododendrons are especially suitable for pots, and can be brought indoors in frosty weather and while in flower.

PLANTING HELP   Plant singly in partial shade and shelter in a well-crocked container approximately 10–16in (25–40cm) wide by 10–12in (25–30cm) deep, in autumn or spring. Dwarf, small-leaved azaleas tend to prefer some sun. Use ericaceous compost, possibly combined with some granulated bark, rotted bracken or

Rhododendron impeditum

An ancient potted azalea growing in a temple courtyard in Sichuan, China

conifer needles. Never allow the pots to dry out. Water well in summer and spray with soft rainwater daily during dry, warm spells. Apply liquid feed monthly during the growing season. Layering is the most successful method of propagation but evergreen azaleas are easy to increase from cuttings, and collecting and growing the seed from deciduous azaleas is a simple, but rather slow alternative. No pruning is necessary but removal of dead flower heads encourages the development of new buds.

'Norma'

Rhododendron 'Countess of Haddington'
A tender rhododendron that grows to about 7ft (2m) tall. Hardy to 20°F (–6°C), US zones 9–10.

Rhododendron yakushimanum
(syn. *R. degronianum* subsp. *yakushimanum*)
A rhododendron that grows to 8ft (2.5m) tall in the wild, but usually makes a low mound in cultivation. Hardy to 0°F (–18°C), US zones 7–10.

Rhododendron 'Norma'   An azalea that grows to 5ft (1.5m) tall with double, scented flowers. Hardy to –20°F (–29°C), US zones 5–9.

Rhododendron impeditum   A dwarf azalea that grows to 3½ft (1m) tall. Hardy to –30°F (–35°C), US zones 4–8.

Rhododendron 'Winsome'   A rhododendron that grows to 5ft (1.5m) tall, bearing leaves that are bronze when young. Hardy to 10°F (–12°C), US zones 8–10.

Tender rhododendron 'Countess of Haddington'

Rhododendron yakushimanum, a good dwarf for pots

Rhododendron 'Winsome'

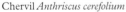

Chervil *Anthriscus cerefolium*

Lovage *Levisticum officinale* in a box parterre at Hollington Nurseries

Herbs

Herbs are a perfect choice for containers, window boxes and planters. Most herbs can be grown in containers but it is wise to confine your choice to smaller plants if space is restricted; plants like lovage and angelica need large pots to grow well, whereas an attractive and sweet-smelling contained herb garden is perfectly possible in a very small area. If you choose those that like the same conditions, it is easy to grow several different herbs in the same pot, where they will make a pleasing combination. Chives, parsley, celery and fennel need good soil, moisture and not too much heat. Thyme, sage, rosemary and lavender all thrive in a dry, hot position. Mints are so powerful that they are best confined by themselves, but several varieties can be planted together. Sorrel can be planted with coriander and cumin in good soil, with partial shade.

Some herbs are annual or biennial, others are herbaceous perennials dying back in winter but reappearing in the following year. Remember, there are often several varieties of the same herb, and sizes and colours can vary considerably.

Thyme

Thymes can be grown in containers outdoors and inside on a sunny windowsill.

PLANTING HELP Thymes generally prefer light, slightly sandy, well-drained soil in a sunny position. Do not overwater, particularly in winter. Most thymes are easily propagated from softwood cuttings taken in the spring, or in the case of a few varieties, from minute seeds. To take cuttings, snip shoots to about 2½–2¾in (6–7cm) and grow on in compost made up of more or less equal parts of peat, sand, bark and grit. All thymes will benefit from a trim after flowering to prevent legginess.

Lemon Thyme *Thymus × citriodorus* A loose bush that grows up to 12in (30cm) tall and 8in (20cm) wide and has broad lemon-scented leaves. Deep pink flowers appear a little later than some of the other thymes. Hardy to 0°F (−18°C), US zones 7–10.

Lemon Thyme *Thymus × citriodorus*

***Thymus* 'Archer's Gold'**
A cultivar with mid-green leaves edged with yellow.

***Thymus* 'Porlock'**
Grows to 12in (30cm) tall with mauve flowers and dark green leaves.

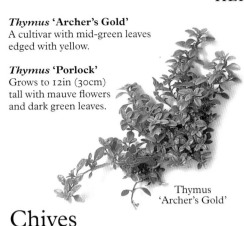

Thymus 'Archer's Gold'

Chives

Allium schoenoprasum A hardy perennial that grows to about 2ft (60cm) tall and has thin grass-like but tubular leaves, smelling of onion. The plant dies down in winter, but re-emerges in spring. Hardy to –30°F (–35°C), US zones 4–8.

PLANTING HELP   Easily grown in good, peaty soil in a sunny or partially shaded position. Water through the summer to keep a good supply of leaves going.

Lovage

Levisticum officinale A handsome, robust perennial found throughout Europe but probably originating from the eastern Mediterranean region. The young shoots are bronze-coloured when they first emerge in early spring and develop into stems up to 7ft (2m) tall, bearing strongly scented, dark green, glossy divided leaves. The small flowers are yellowish green, borne in clusters in summer and are followed by ovoid brown fruits. The plant smells overpoweringly of celery. It also tastes like celery but with a distinct yeastiness. Hardy to –30°F (–35°C), US zones 4–8.

PLANTING HELP   Lovage can be grown from ripe seed sown outside in the autumn, or dried seed indoors in the spring; alternatively, divide and replant the fleshy rootstocks in spring. Grow in sun or semi-shade in good, deep, well-drained, moisture-retaining compost and mulch with manure if you can. It needs a large pot, although it will probably need trimming back as it is apt to become rather untidy. Hardy to 10°F (–12°C), US zones 8–10.

Chervil

Anthriscus cerefolium An annual that grows to about 2ft (60cm) tall and has sweetly aromatic, bright green feathery leaves and clusters of small white flowers. Hardy to 10°F (–12°C), US zones 8–10. Native to S Europe and W Asia.

PLANTING HELP   Sow seed *in situ* (chervil dislikes being transplanted) in moisture-retaining but not waterlogged soil, in succession from spring through summer to provide a continuous supply of fresh young leaves. Chervil should not be allowed to dry out, as the plants will 'bolt' into seed very quickly. It can be grown in pots either indoors or out, and can therefore be brought indoors for the winter.

Thymus 'Porlock'   Chives *Allium schoenoprasum*

25

Marjoram 'Gold Tip'   Spearmint *Mentha spicata*

Basil

Common, **Genovese** or **Sweet Basil** *Ocimum basilicum*   Depending on climate, this species can be either an annual bushy plant that grows to about 12in (30cm), or a perennial that eventually reaches about 3½ft (1m) high. The strongly scented leaves are a glossy, light green and the flowers are white, sometimes tinged with pale purple. Hardy to 32°F (0°C), US zone 10.

O. basilicum **'Neapolitanum'** Lettuce-leaved Basil   Grows to about 18in (45cm) and is similar to the common Sweet Basil, but has much larger leaves and a slightly stronger flavour. It needs ample sun and warmth. Snip off the leaf tips for cooking and cut off any shoots that are about to flower as this will keep the plant producing healthy leaves for longer.

PLANTING HELP   Sow seed in a warm place in early spring. After germinating (which takes 2–3 weeks) they can be grown on until large enough to handle; water sparingly in the morning only. Transplant the seedlings into small pots and gradually harden off; do not be tempted to plant them outside until all risk of frost has passed. Plant them in well-drained compost with some sand or grit and water carefully and place in a really warm, sheltered position. We have found the purple

Sweet Basil

and more tropical basils (*not illustrated*) much trickier to grow and even more liable to damping off than the common green variety. Careful watering is important if they are to make good-sized plants.

Lemon Balm

Melissa officinalis **'Aurea'** Variegated Lemon Balm   A perennial native to S Europe and found naturalized elsewhere, growing to 3ft (90cm) tall, producing small, whitish yellow flowers during summer and early autumn. The variegated variety has green leaves splashed with cream. Beware, this plant seeds itself very freely and the seedlings may revert to the unvariegated form. Hardy to 0°F (–18°C), US zones 7–10.

PLANTING HELP   Plant in any reasonable compost in sun or shade, although it prefers a dry well-drained site and is actually quite drought-resistant. Trim back continuously to ensure a steady supply of young leaves. Propagate by division in the spring.

Marjoram

Origanum vulgare **'Gold Tip'** (syn. *O.* 'Variegatum')   A bushy perennial with spreading stems that grow to 16in (40cm), bearing aromatic, curly green leaves tipped with yellow and producing clusters of pinky white flowers, surrounded by purple tinted green bracts, which look like outer petals. Hardy to 0°F (–18°C), US zones 7–10.

HERBS

PLANTING HELP   Plant in well-drained, dry compost in full sun. Can be grown from seed, sown thinly as the seed is very fine, in spring, preferably with some bottom heat and kept only slightly moist. Pot on once the seedlings are big enough to handle. Put them in pots outside when the weather is warm enough.

Mint

There are numerous species of mint which can be grown in pots. The diversity of scents together with the number of greens, gold- and white-variegated forms is quite surprising. Most mints are creeping plants which spread freely if given the chance and therefore the restriction of containers suits them very well.

PLANTING HELP   Plant in rich, warm, well-drained compost in partial shade, where the soil will not dry out quickly. Propagate by pulling off rooted runners and replanting where required. Mint usually fails to thrive after a few years and small rooted pieces should be replanted in fresh compost. Mildew and rust can be a problem, but

it is unwise to spray culinary plants; instead, cut off the affected shoots and burn them. In our experience these diseases will disappear by the next spring.

Spearmint *Mentha spicata*   The best mint, if you have room for only one. This grows to about 2ft (75cm) tall, bearing sweet-smelling, bright green leaves and lilac pink flowers, much visited by bees and butterflies during summer and early autumn. Hardy to −10°F (−23°C), US zones 6–9.

Lettuce-leaved Basil

Variegated Lemon Balm

27

Scabiosa 'Butterfly Blue'

Scabious

***Scabiosa* 'Butterfly Blue'** A form or hybrid of
S. columbaria which is an herbaceous perennial,
native to Europe including England and Wales,
where it grows on chalk and limestone hills. Stems
are 2¼ft (70cm) tall, bearing grey green leaves and
producing lavender blue flower heads in mid- to
late summer. Wonderful for attracting butterflies.
Hardy to −10°F (−23°C), US zones 6–9.

PLANTING HELP   Plant in full sun in any
reasonable, slightly alkaline potting compost and
protect from excess wet in winter. Dead-head to
prolong flowering. Divide and replant with fresh
compost every 3 years or so. Sow seed in spring.

Sedum

The late-flowering herbaceous sedums produce
short stems with fleshy leaves and flat heads of tiny
flowers that attract every butterfly in the garden.
They are ideal plants for a sunny position.

PLANTING HELP   For any good soil. Plant in
spring and propagate by division. Water in dry
summers as these large-leaved sedums are not as
drought-tolerant as the dwarf stonecrops.

Sedum 'Sunset Cloud'

***Sedum spectabile* 'Carmen'** A clump-
forming perennial with stems to 2¼ft (70cm) tall,
and flower heads to 5in (12cm) across, in late
summer and autumn. Hardy to −10°F (−23°C),
US zones 6–9.

***Sedum* 'Sunset Cloud'**   A hybrid of *Sedum
telephium*, a rare native of dry woods in Britain, N
Europe and Asia. Leaves purplish grey; sprawling
stems to 1ft (30cm), topped by rounded clusters of
flowers. Hardy to −10°F (−23°C), US zones 6–9.

Lavender

Aromatic evergreen shrubs and sub-shrubs from
the Mediterranean region, attractive for their
flowers and foliage.

PLANTING HELP   For any reasonable potting
mix in full sun; lavenders actually flower more
profusely in pots which are slightly too small. Sow
seed in containers in spring or take semi-ripe
cuttings in summer.

English Lavender *Lavandula augustifolia*
'Hidcote'   A densely branched shrub that grows
2–2½ft (60–75cm) tall, producing bluish violet
flower spikes ⅓in (1cm) long in early summer.
Hardy to 0°F (−18°C), US zones 7–10.

Sedum spectabile 'Carmen' with
small tortoiseshell butterflies

French Lavender *Lavandula stoechas* A shrub that grows to 3ft (90cm) tall, bearing short stalks of small, deep purple flowers over-topped by distinctive purple bracts, about 1½in (4cm) long, in early summer.

Phuyopsis

Phuyopsis stylosa A creeping perennial with spreading stems to 1ft (30cm) and whorls of narrow leaves, topped by heads of small purplish pink flowers which are much loved by butterflies. The whole plant has a characteristic pungent smell. Hardy to –10°F (–23°C), US zones 6–9.

PLANTING HELP For any soil in sun or part shade. Plant in spring and propagate by division; may become invasive in good soil.

English Lavender *Lavandula augustifolia*

Lavender 'Hidcote'

French Lavender

Phuyopsis stylosa with *Geranium sanguineum* and rockroses between paving at Barnsley House

Dianthus showing grey foliage in St Ives, Cornwall

Alpines

Most alpines are dwarf, compact plants which need good drainage and are particularly happy among rocks in stone troughs pots and sinks.

Saxifraga

The dwarf saxifrages are among the prettiest and most satisfactory alpines for a trough, sink or large pot. Many do well planted into holes in a large piece of tufa rock and a collection can make a miniature garden of its own.

PLANTING HELP   Plant in moist, well-drained, rich compost in shade. Sow seed in containers in autumn. Divide individual rosettes and root in late spring or early summer. Aphids and slugs may damage these plants and vine weevil grubs eat the roots.

Saxifraga 'Garnet'   A hybrid mat-forming plant bearing deep pink flowers in spring above crowded rosettes of soft moss-like leaves. Mossy saxifrages grow among damp rocks, mainly in the mountains of western Europe. Hardy to −20°F (−29°C), US zones 5–9.

London Pride *Saxifraga × urbium*   A hybrid between *S. spathularis* St Patrick's Cabbage from western Ireland, and *S. umbrosa* from the Pyrenees. It is popular in shady, urban gardens and is a spreading plant that grows to 1ft (30cm) tall, with large rosettes of toothed, leathery leaves, each ¾–1½in (2–4cm) long, and loose clusters of minute star-shaped, white, pink-spotted flowers in summer. Hardy to 0°F (−18°C), US zones 7–10.

Pinks

All pinks are well known for their wonderful scent, but there are several dwarf varieties of *Dianthus* which are ideal for window boxes and containers. Alpine pinks form mats or cushions of grey foliage, with pink or red flowers.

PLANTING HELP   All prefer a limy soil, sharp drainage and full sun. Be careful not to bury the lowest leaves when planting. Remove flower stems after flowering to encourage a second flowering the same year. Sow seed in containers from autumn to early spring.

Dianthus 'Inshriach Dazzler'   An alpine perennial that grows to 4in (10cm) tall, bearing

flowers 1in (2.5cm) across, in early summer.
Hardy to -10°F (-23°C), US zones 6–9.

Dianthus 'Musgrave's Pink' A well scented
double variety, bred in 1730.

Bellflower

Campanula portenschlagiana A mound-
forming evergreen perennial that grows to 6in
(15cm) tall, with small heart-shaped leaves and
clusters of bell-shaped, purple flowers ¾in (2cm)
long, in mid- to late summer. Native to mountains
in Croatia. Hardy to -30°F (-35°C), US zones
4–8. Many small campanulas are suitable for
growing in containers; some of the spreading or
clump-forming rock-garden species, such as this,
are perfect candidates for planting between paving
slabs and stones, or in low walls.

PLANTING HELP Plant in moist, well-
drained compost in sun or light shade. Sow seed in
autumn. Divide clumps in spring or autumn. May
attract slugs and snails.

Oenothera

Evening Primrose *Oenothera speciosa* 'Siskiyou'
A spreading herbaceous perennial with flowering
stems that grow to 1ft (30cm) tall, bearing a
succession of large pink flowers with yellow eyes,
deeper pink as they fade, each 3in (8cm) wide.
Hardy to -20°F (-29°C), US zones 5–9. There are
several other pink varieties of the normally white
Oenothera speciosa.

PLANTING HELP For full sun in any rich and
fertile alpine potting mix, possibly among rocks or
stones. Keep dry in winter. Sow seed in containers
in early spring. Divide in early spring. Slugs may
eat these plants.

Oenothera speciosa 'Siskiyou'

Bellflower *Campanula portenschlagiana*

London Pride *Saxifraga × urbium*

Saxifraga 'Garnet' at the Denver
Botanical Gardens, Colorado

Dianthus 'Inshriach Dazzler'

Dianthus 'Musgrave's Pink'

A good mixed pot with *Diascia*, *Helichrysum petiolare* 'Variegatum', *Verbena*, *Sutera* 'Knysna Hills', orange and red *Mimulus glutinosus* and a striped *Phormium*

Tender Perennials

Just as grey foliage perennials provide the background to container planting, so tender flowering perennials can provide the colour, a role often taken by annuals too. These tender perennials are becoming more popular every year. They are easily propagated from cuttings, or sometimes by tissue culture, and are sold in the garden centres as small plants in spring. They should be put into larger pots as soon as they are brought home, and carefully hardened off,

Nolana
'Shooting Star'

before planting out when danger of frost and icy winds has passed. They will then grow rapidly and flower throughout the summer, provided they are well watered and fertilized regularly.

Most of these perennials do not set seed, so will continue to flower longer than annuals. They need propagating by cuttings in late summer, and overwintering under glass.

Diascia

A genus of 50 or so annuals and perennials, native to South Africa, where most grow in moist, grassy places in the mountains. They are often grown in pots, window boxes and hanging baskets, and are easy and free-flowering throughout the summer. Hardy to 10°F (−12°C), US zones 8–10.

PLANTING HELP   Plant in any reasonable potting mix in full sun, and water well throughout the summer. Sow seed when ripe, in warmth in early spring. Take cuttings at any time of year.

Diascia 'Sydney Olympics' in a hanging basket

Diascia barberae **'Salmon Supreme'** (syn.
D. 'Hector Harrison') A mat-forming perennial
that grows to 6in (15cm) tall, although it can grow
taller in beds, bearing heart-shaped leaves 1–1½in
(2.5–4cm) long, and producing clusters of peachy
pink flowers ½in (1.5cm) long into autumn.

Diascia **'Sydney Olympics'** A sprawling
perennial which will grow to 15in (40cm) tall,
bearing masses of pink flowers with dark centres.

Nolana

A small genus of tender annuals and perennials
from Chile to Peru. They make very good plants
for hanging baskets.

PLANTING HELP Sow seed *in situ* just below
the surface in full sun. For early-flowering plants,
sow seed in early spring at about 60°F (16°C),
transplant to 3in (8cm) diameter pots and finally
transplant into larger containers. Water freely
during growth and feed monthly.

Diascia barberae 'Salmon Supreme'

Nolana humifusa **'Shooting Star'** Long
trailing stems bearing masses of bell-shaped
flowers. Wonderful for trailing from containers or
hanging baskets. Hardy to 32°F (0°C), US zone 10.

Nolana paradoxa **'Blue Bird'** A perennial
usually grown as an annual, 6–8in (15–20cm) tall.
Wonderful for a window box and hanging basket,
with creeping stems bearing masses of light blue,
bell-shaped flowers with creamy throats. Hardy to
32°F (0°C), US zone 10.

Nolana paradoxa 'Blue Bird'

33

Calceolaria integrifolia 'Midas' with fuchsias, petunias, lobelias and red pelargoniums in a window box

Calceolaria integrifolia 'Midas'

Calceolaria

***Calceolaria integrifolia* 'Midas'**
An evergreen sub-shrubby perennial usually grown as an annual, to 10in (25cm) tall, bearing deep yellow flowers in early summer. The Latin name for this plant is taken from the word *calceolus* meaning *slipper* or *little shoe* which describes the strangely shaped flowers. Although a great favourite in Victorian times, calceolarias are no longer as popular as they were in the past. However, the pouched flowers are bright and colourful and provide an attractive display throughout the summer in tubs, window boxes and hanging baskets. Hardy to 32°F (0°C), US zone 10.

PLANTING HELP   Plant in full sun or partial shade in any reasonable, slightly acid potting mix. Water well when in growth and apply liquid feed every few weeks.

Lysimachia

***Lysimachia henryi* 'Sunset'**   A herb producing trailing stems to 12in (30cm) long, bearing thick, variegated leaves and clusters of star-shaped, yellow flowers. Native to China. Hardy to 10°F (−12°C), US zones 8–10, perhaps. Wonderful in hanging baskets, window boxes and containers.

PLANTING HELP   Plant in rich, moist, well-drained compost in full sun or partial shade. Sow seed in containers outdoors in spring.

Lysimachia henryi 'Sunset'

Nemesia strumosa mixed colours

Sutera campanulata 'Knysna Hills'

Nemesia

Showy, two-lipped
flowers in various
colours, including
some bicoloured
cultivars, grown
mainly as half-hardy
annuals and making
wonderful container plants.
The perennial species such
as *N. caerulea* need the same
treatment as *Diascia*. Hardy to
20°F (–6°C), US zones 9–10.

PLANTING HELP   Plant in full
sun in well-drained, slightly acidic
compost. Keep well watered to
prolong flowering and pinch out
growing tips to encourage bushy
plants. Sow seed in warmth in spring
for summer-flowering plants, or in
autumn for container plants in spring.

Nemesia
'KLM'

Nemesia strumosa   An erect annual herb
growing 6–24in (15–60cm) tall, bearing leaves to
2¾in (7cm) long, and producing loose clusters of
two-lipped red, yellow, pink, blue, purple, white or
bicoloured flowers from midsummer to autumn.
Native to South Africa.

Nemesia versicolor   An annual herb that
grows to 20in (50cm) tall, bearing leaves 2in
(5cm) long, and producing clusters of two-lipped
blue, mauve, yellow, white or bicoloured flowers in
mid- to late summer; the lower lip is longer and
wider than the top petal. ' KLM' is a selection.

Sutera

A genus of small shrubs, sub-shrubs and
perennials that are rather tender and thus
normally grown as annuals in temperate regions,
however, they can be overwintered in a heated
greenhouse. They come from South Africa.

PLANTING HELP   Plant in full sun in well-
drained compost. Water freely during growth and
feed monthly. Root cuttings in late summer, with
bottom heat.

Sutera campanulata 'Knysna Hills'   A dwarf
bushy perennial with stems that grow to 18in
(45cm) long, sticky leaves and masses of small,
pale mauve flowers. Native to South Africa,
flowering throughout summer and in mild seasons
into early winter. Leaves toothed, ¾in (1.5cm)
long; flowers around ½in (1.5cm) across. Hardy to
32°F (0°C), US zone 10.

Sutera cordata 'Snowflake'
A creeping perennial with rounded
few-toothed leaves and masses of
small white flowers. Native to
South Africa, flowering all the
year in the wild. Leaves around
½in (1.5cm); flowers around ½in
(1.5cm) across. This is
sold for planting
in hanging
baskets,
commonly
called *Bacopa* by
mistake. Hardy to 32°F
(0°C), US zone 10.

Sutera cordata
'Snowflake'

Trailing *Lobelia richardsonii* in a tall pot

Laurentia axillaris

Cascade lobelia 'Lilac' in a hanging basket

Lobelias and *Asteriscus* in pots

Lobelia

Lobelia is a genus of annuals, perennials and shrubs from tropical and temperate areas throughout the world. Their wild habitat varies considerably; lobelias can be found in woodlands and on mountain slopes, in dry areas but more often in marshes, wet meadows and on riverbanks. All have simple, often stalkless leaves and narrow-tubed flowers with two lips, the lower lip usually larger and 3-lobed.

Mixed trailing lobelias

The annuals are particularly suitable for hanging baskets, window boxes and for trailing down the side of pots and containers. The cultivars of *Lobelia erinus* are usually grown as annuals. Most are low-growing, bushy or trailing in habit, producing masses of blue, purple, red, pink or white flowers, often with yellow or white

Trailing lobelia with a fuchsia at Powis Castle

Scaevola aemula 'Blue Fan'

centres, from summer to autumn. There are several series of cultivars which have different characteristics: for example, those of the Moon series flower very early in the season, as do those of the Regata and Riviera series; the Pendula or Cascade series are excellent for pot use.

The Fountain series was bred specifically to feed the increasing demand for new trailing varieties suitable for hanging baskets. It has large flowers and broad-leaved foliage, flowering early in the season. There are several different colours available. *L. richardsonii* is a species with light blue flowers on trailing stems.

Cascades of lobelias can look superb in hanging baskets, window boxes and patio tubs, forming a spectacular framework for other plants and providing a tumbling florescence to dissipate the angular appearance of the container itself.

PLANTING HELP   Lobelias vary in tenderness although the annuals referred to above are generally half-hardy, withstanding temperatures down to about 0°F (32°C), US zone 10. Plants benefit from being watered before planting and again afterwards. Place 6in (15cm) apart in sun or partial shade, feed every few weeks and remove dead flower heads to prolong flowering. Seeds of annuals should be sown in late winter. It is important to keep compost moist; enthusiasm in this respect, particularly before the plants have become established, will ensure the best results.

Laurentia

Laurentia axillaris **'Blue Stars'**   This bushy perennial and some other closely related species from Australia have been selected especially for containers and hanging baskets. Their slender flower stems emerge from a dome of narrow foliage bearing night-scented starry flowers to 1in (2.5cm) across. Colours are pale blue in *L. axillaris* 'Blue Stars', white in *L.* 'Shooting Stars' and pink in *L.* 'Starlight Pink'. 'Stargazer' is a mixture of all three colours. Hardy to 32°F (0°C), US zone 10.

PLANTING HELP   For full sun in a sandy potting mix. Sow seeds before the end of January to ensure flowering plants from July onwards.

Scaevola

Scaevola aemula **'Blue Fan'** Fairy Fan Flower Another Australian evergreen perennial that grows to 20in (50cm) tall, bearing roundish, toothed leaves to 3½in (9cm) long and distinctive fan-shaped flowers. These plants can be grown in any zone but will be killed by the first frost.

PLANTING HELP   Plant in full sun or light shade. Water freely during growth and feed monthly. Sow seed in warmth in spring. Root cuttings in late spring or summer, with heat.

Verbena 'Pink Parfait' with lobelias and variegated pelargoniums in a window box

Verbena

A genus of 200–300 perennials and annuals widely distributed throughout the American continents, although a few are native to S Europe. The modern cultivars of *V.* × *hybrida* make ideal plants for window boxes, planters, containers and hanging baskets.

Verbena 'Novalis Rose Pink'

PLANTING HELP   Sow seed or buy young plants in spring and plant seedlings outside in late May in any reasonable potting compost in a sunny position. Pinching out the tips of young plants will produce a more attractive plant. Unlike many other tender perennials, the flowers of the verbena die tidily and therefore do not usually need dead-heading. Water well in dry weather.

Verbena* × *hybrida (syn. *V. hortensis*)   A group of bushy, upright, spreading or mat-forming perennials which are usually grown as annuals, bearing stems to about 18in (45cm) long. In

Verbena with variegated *Helichrysum petiolare*

VERBENA

summer and autumn they produce clusters, 3in (8cm) or so in width, of sometimes scented, tiny white, red, pink, purple or yellow flowers with white centres. Hardy to 20°F (–6°C), US zone 9–10.

Verbena **'Pink Parfait'** A sprawling perennial bearing pink flowers. Hardy to 32°F (0°C), US zone 10.

Verbena **'Arrow Pink'** A sprawling perennial bearing strong pink flowers. Hardy to 32°F (0°C), US zone 10.

Verbena **'Imagination'** (syn. *V. speciosa* 'Imagination') A spreading cultivar which forms mounds and bears violet flowers; it is particularly recommended for hanging baskets.

The Novalis Series These cultivars are upright and bushy, to 10in (25cm) tall, with rounded

flower heads of white-centred and single-coloured blooms in a variety of pinks, reds and blues.

The Romance Series These cultivars are upright and bushy, to 10in (25cm) tall, producing white-centred or single-coloured blooms in a variety of whites, deep reds and pinks.

Verbena rigida (syn. *V. venosa*) A perennial often grown as an annual, bearing erect and spreading stems 18–24in (45–60cm) long, producing clusters of fragrant, pink purple flowers in summer. Native to South America. Hardy to 20°F (–6°C), US zones 9–10.

Verbena canadensis **'Perfecta'** (syn. *V. aublieta* 'Perfecta') A plant that grows to 8in (20cm) tall, producing showy clusters of deep violet flowers over a long period in summer. Hardy to –30°F(–35°C), US zones 4–8.

Verbena 'Arrow Pink'

Verbena 'Romance Lavender'

Verbena 'Imagination' (*left*), *Verbena rigida* (*centre*) and *Verbena canadensis* 'Perfecta' (*right*)

Pelargoniums & Geraniums

Pelargonium 'Voodoo'

There is often confusion between geraniums and pelargoniums, some of the latter sometimes being referred to as geraniums. *Pelargonium* is a genus of evergreen or deciduous perennials and shrubs, mainly from South Africa, hybridized in Europe since the early 18th century. *Geranium* is a genus of mostly hardy herbaceous perennials, found worldwide. *Pelargonium* cultivars can be classified into half a dozen groups, several of which are illustrated here. There is a great range of varieties available and new cultivars are produced every year. Hardy to 32°F (0°C), US zone 10.

PLANTING HELP   Seeds are sown in early spring under glass at a temperature of about 60°F (15°C). They should be potted up prior to hardening off, and can be planted out in early summer. Cuttings can also be taken in the summer or early autumn, to overwinter for the following year.

Zonal Pelargoniums   Often referred to as geraniums, these plants are extremely popular and are seen in gardens, greenhouses, window boxes, balconies and windowsills everywhere. They grow to 1–1½ft (30–45cm) tall in a season, bearing rounded leaves, often with a dark bronze zone from which their name is derived, and they have single or double flowers, 1–2in (2.5–5cm) wide, of white, pink, salmon, red or purple, borne in large clusters.
Pelargonium **'Mrs Parker'**   Grows to 18in (45cm) tall, bearing variegated leaves and producing flowers to 1in (2.5cm) wide, in summer.
Pelargonium **'Stellar Apricot'**   This cultivar belongs to the Stellar series, one of several subgroups of the Zonal pelargonium hybrids, the flowers of which are irregularly star-shaped. The first Stellar was raised in Australia by Ted Both of Adelaide in around 1965; 'Stella Apricot' has very dainty, well-marked leaves with pointed lobes and slender umbels of pretty apricot flowers.

Ivy-leaved Pelargoniums   These are trailing plants with rather thick, glossy leaves, derived from *Pelargonium peltatum*, first introduced into Holland in a consignment of plants sent by the governor of Cape Province in 1700. This group is particularly good for hanging baskets, tubs and clothing trelliswork. The leaves are 1–5in (2.5–12cm) across and somewhat resemble those of ivy. They bear clusters of single or double flowers 1½in (4cm) wide in shades of red, pink, mauve, purple or white.
Pelargonium **'Decora Rose'**   A plant with trailing growth to 1ft (30cm), bearing clusters of flowers, each 1¼in (3cm) wide, in summer. Hardy to 32°F (0°C), US zone 10.
Pelargonium peltatum   Grows wild in the Cape Province of South Africa, where it scrambles through vegetation up to 7ft (2m). Flowers mauve to pale pink or white.

Ivy-leaved Pelargoniums with *Helichrysum*

Pelargonium 'Askam Fringed Aztec'

Ivy-leaved geraniums at Sangerhausen

Regal Pelargoniums   Shrubby plants with jagged-edged leaves 2–4in (5–10cm) long, and large, bicoloured, ruffled flowers, usually single but occasionally semi-double, 1½in (4cm) wide, in red, pink, purple, peach or white. Modern hybrids can be made to flower all summer indoors but need a warm sheltered site outdoors.
Pelargonium **'Askam Fringed Aztec'** (syn. *P.* 'Betty Bly')   A compact plant with a finely incised petal edge.

Unique Pelargoniums   Shrubby evergreen perennials with rounded, sometimes lobed, leaves 2–5in (5–12cm) across, which produce a characteristic scent when rubbed, bearing clusters of flowers in shades of white, pink, red, purple or peach, to 1¼in (3cm) across.
Pelargonium **'Aurore'**   Grows to 20–24in (50–60cm) tall, bearing clusters 4in (10cm) wide, of deep pink flowers with dark spots on the top petals. Leaves softly hairy.
Pelargonium **'Voodoo'**   Grows to 20–24in (50–60cm) tall, bearing clusters 3in (8cm) wide, of deep red flowers with deep purple centres. This plant can be grown in any zone but will not withstand much frost.

Geranium

Geranium dalmaticum   A dwarf, creeping evergreen perennial that grows to 6in (15cm) tall, bearing rosettes of glossy, divided leaves 1½in (4cm) long, and clusters of pink flowers 1–1½in (2.5–4cm) wide with red anthers, on long stalks in summer. Native to E Europe. Hardy to 10°F (–12°C), US zones 8–10. Geraniums are relatively undemanding plants which are easily grown and attractive in pots and containers.

PLANTING HELP
Plant in any reasonably fertile potting compost in full sun or partial shade. Water freely in growing season and fertilize monthly. Water sparingly in winter and remove flowering stems and old leaves. Sow seed in containers outdoors in spring. Propagate from cuttings in spring and root with bottom heat.

Pelargonium peltatum

41

Pelargonium 'Decora Rose'

Geranium dalmaticum in an ancient stone bowl

A good group of 'Stellar Apricot' in a fine pot

Pelargonium 'Mrs Parker'

Pelargonium 'Decora Impérial' in Tuscany

PELARGONIUMS & GERANIUMS

Potted zonal pelargoniums trained on bamboos

Pelargoniums in Mexico   *Pelargonium* 'Pink Aurore'

43

New Guinea *Impatiens* 'Ambience'

Impatiens Accent Series

Impatiens 'Double Diamond Rose'

Busy Lizzie

The Latin name *Impatiens* refers to the way the seed pods of most species, seemingly impatiently, burst and scatter their seed when touched. There are about 500 different wild species, native to the mountainous areas of Asia and Africa, and a few in North America. Many are annuals, others perennials with corms, tubers or fleshy roots and many are sub-shrubs. Numerous cultivars have been raised.

New Guinea Series 'Isis'

Thanks in part to the countless special offers in newspapers and magazines, and to the efforts of hybridizers, busy lizzies are freely available and have become the definitive container plant for summer. They are easy to grow provided they have enough water and shade for part of the day. They provide a dazzling display of colour, either alone or mixed with other plants. A few containers full can transform an entire garden with very little effort and they are particularly effective in shady corners.

For many years busy lizzies were thought of as house plants; the Victorians placed them on

Mixed New Guinea *Impatiens*

IMPATIENS

Pots of *Impatiens* in Princeton, New Jersey

windowsills rather than in window boxes and hanging baskets. However, breeding programmes worldwide have led to the development of the prolific flowering varieties now available.

Impatiens walleriana The species from which many of the modern cultivars have been developed, this is a very leafy plant, but in modern cultivars the leaves are almost hidden by the large flowers.

Super Elfin Series Spreading plants with flat flowers in a wide colour range that grow to 10in (25cm) tall. These plants can be grown in any zone but will be killed by the first frost.

Accent Series Cultivars that have compact flowers, some with star-shaped centres, in a variety of colours including white. Growing to 8in (20cm) tall, these plants can be grown in any zone but will be killed by the first frost.

New Guinea Impatiens Derived from *I. hawkeri* from New Guinea, these sub-shrubby hybrid perennials are usually grown as annuals, valued for their large brightly coloured flowers and attractive bronze-tinted or variegated foliage. To 10in (25cm) tall, these plants can be grown in any zone but will be killed by the first frost.

PLANTING HELP Plant in a peaty potting mix in sun or partial shade. Impatiens seeds need heat to germinate and make their initial growth; cuttings also root quite easily. Seedlings and plugs are readily available at very reasonable prices, so that only real enthusiasts will attempt to raise their own. Keep plants well watered. While there are impatiens that are hardy to 10°F (−12°C), US zones 8–10, most are frost-tender, losing their leaves in temperatures below 40°F (5°C), the warmer parts of zone 10.

Impatiens 'Accent White' with *Verbena* 'Imagination'

45

Petunias

Although they are usually grown as annuals, petunias are actually perennials from rocky slopes, steppes and disturbed ground in South America. There are approximately 40 different wild species but many more cultivars have been bred for garden use. Until recently, there were two main groups: Grandiflora and Multiflora, but a third group has now been added, the Milliflora group, which has increased the diversity of cultivars available.

'Million Bells'

As their respective names suggest, the Grandiflora has bigger flowers, up to 4in (10cm) wide, and the Multiflora is bushier with a greater profusion of smaller flowers, up to 2in (5cm) wide. The birth of the Milliflora series has heralded the arrival of a much smaller-flowered plant, the blooms being only a third the size of those of a Grandiflora cultivar. As a general rule, Grandiflora petunias benefit from being grown in pots and containers because of their vulnerability to rain damage, whereas both the Multiflora and Milliflora petunias are more tolerant of water on the flowers.

Petunia 'Million Bells'   This is a recent introduction with masses of very small flowers about 1in (2.5cm) across, and a trailing, slightly woody habit, perfect for hanging baskets. The flowers last from midsummer to the first frosts.

The **Surfinia Series**   Grow 9–16in (23–40cm) tall and are particularly useful in hanging baskets because of their long trailing habit. They are sterile and usually propagated by cuttings.

The **Daddy Series**   Grow to 14in (35cm) tall, and are early-flowering Grandiflora cultivars in a range of colours, usually with much veining.

The **Fantasy Series**   Milliflora cultivars covered with countless flowers, each about 1½in (4cm) across, and lasting throughout the summer. The plants are 8–10in (20–25cm) tall and are available in six different colours.

The **Horizon Series**   Multifloras which have flowers of many colours, often with a pale throat.

The **Primetime Series**   Multiflora cultivars which have flowers of many colours, some with dark veins or central stars.

The **Ultra Series**   Grandiflora cultivars which have large flowers in a range of colours, often with central stars.

PLANTING HELP   Sow seeds in warmth. Plant 4–6in (10–15cm) apart in any well-drained potting mix during the coolest part of the day in a sunny, sheltered position. Feed after planting to help prevent transplant shock and keep well watered to ensure an abundance of flowers. Removal of dead flowers prolongs flowering. Protect from frost. Hardy to 0°F (32°C), US zone 10. Petunias can also be propagated from cuttings.

Petunia Fantasy series 'Pink' in a basket on a stand and as bedding

PETUNIAS

Surfinia petunias in a basket with tuberous begonias, pelargoniums, trailing lobelias and ground ivy

PETUNIAS

Petunia Surfinia Series 'Purple Mini'

Petunia Horizon Series 'Horizon Yellow'

Petunia Surfinia Series 'Pink Vein'

Petunia 'Blue Daddy'

Petunia 'Primetime' and 'Blue Star'

Petunia 'Pastel Pink' (*left*), 'Purple' (*centre*) and 'Violet Blue' (*right*)

Surfinia petunias are perfect for hanging baskets, seen here in Eccleston Square

Geraniums and Surfinia petunias with fuchsia on steps in Penzance

Nicotiana 'Havana Lime Green' grown in plastic trays and cleverly put on an old stone box

Flowering Tobacco

There are around 60 species of *Nicotiana* annuals, perennials, shrubs and small trees, native to America, with one or two species in Australia. The genus is named aftern Jean Nicot (1530–1600) French consul to Portugal, who introduced tobacco to France. Smoking tobacco, *N. tabacum*, has large leaves and rather small tubular flowers. The main flowering tobacco, *N. alata* was popular in Victorian tropical bedding schemes.

Unlike the original wild varieties, modern cultivars produce flowers that remain open during the day and there are many dwarf varieties available which make superb container plants, being decorative in appearance, sweetly smelling, in a range of colours and easily grown.

PLANTING HELP Plant in rich, well-drained compost in sun or partial shade. Sow seed indoors in moist but not wet compost from late winter to early spring; they need warmth to germinate, but once the seedlings are large enough to handle they can be transplanted and grown on in cooler conditions. It is a good idea to acclimatize seedlings gradually to outdoor conditions before planting out after all frosts have passed.

Nicotiana × sanderae Several series of popular garden cultivars originate from this plant, a hybrid of *N. alata*, raised in 1903. It grows to 24in (60cm) tall, bearing clusters of red, white, pink or purple flowers 2in (5cm) across. Hardy to 0°F (−18°C), US zones 7–10. The flowers have a sweet scent, most noticeable in the evening; excellent for patio pots or window boxes, where this can be appreciated.

Domino Series Dwarf plants that grow 10–12in (25–30cm) tall, which are heat- and shade-tolerant and bear outward-facing flowers in a variety of pastel colours including lime green and white. Hardy to 10°F (−12°C), US zones 8–10.

Havana Series Dwarf plants that grow 10–12in (25–30cm) tall, which are heat- and shade-tolerant

Nicotiana 'Domino Red'

Nicotiana 'Domino Lime'

Nicotiana 'Appleblossom' and salvias at Kew

Nicotiana 'Sensation Mixed'

Nicotiana × *sanderae*

and available in various shades of pink, red, green and white, with some bicolours. Hardy to 10°F (−12°C), US zones 8–10.

Sensation Series   These grow 2–3ft (60–90cm) tall, bearing flowers in a range of colours including pink, red and white. Hardy to 0°F (−18°C), US zones 7–10.

Nasturtiums with trailing petunias

Tropaeolum majus 'Alaska' in Eccleston Square

Nasturtiums

The Latin name *Nasturtium* is derived from the Latin *nāsus* meaning 'nose' and *tortus* meaning 'twisted', referring to the way one's nose is wrinkled by the pungent smell of the wild species. By a further twist, the Latin name *Nasturtium* was given to the ordinary Watercress. *Tropaeolum majus*, sometimes called Indian Cress, because it came from the West Indies, came to be called Nasturtium in error. These attractive plants have been popular since Victorian times, but showier, colourful cultivars have now supplanted the wild types and there are many wonderfully scented varieties available for pots, containers and hanging baskets. As a bonus, the leaves can be used to add piquancy to summer

'Empress of India'

salads. Cultivars of the annual *Tropaelum majus* are diverse in habit, ranging from climbers that grow to 6ft (1.8m) to the dwarf varieties illustrated here. Hardy to 32°F (0°C), US zones 10.

PLANTING HELP   Sow seeds outdoors from April to May, where they are to flower. Containers should be at least 10in (25cm) wide by 8in (20cm) deep. Seeds of dwarf varieties should be sown ¼in (0.5cm) deep and seedlings thinned out to leave 6in (15cm) between plants. Place in well-drained, poor compost in full sun for best results; nasturtiums produce less flowers when shaded. Water well after planting and again the following week, but thereafter only sparingly. Seeds can be sown indoors in early spring to produce early-flowering plants. Caterpillars and blackfly can cause problems but beware, many nasturiums are intolerant of systemic insecticides which turn their leaves yellow.

***Tropaeolum majus* 'Alaska'**   Grows up to 8in (20cm) tall. Flowers are freely produced in several bright colours. They stand well above the distinctive foliage, which is light green speckled with white. Comes true to seed.

NASTURTIUMS

'Tip Top Apricot'

'Tip Top Scarlet'

Tropaeolum majus 'Alaska' with *Sphaeralcea munroana* at Levens Hall

'Whirlybird Gold'

***Tropaeolum majus* 'Tip Top Scarlet'**
A compact, single-flowered variety that grows 8–10in (20–25cm) tall, producing scarlet blooms well above the foliage.

***Tropaeolum majus* 'Tip Top Apricot'**
A compact, single-flowered variety that grows 8–10in (20–25cm) tall, producing apricot blooms well above the foliage.

***Tropaeolum majus* 'Whirlybird Gold'**   This cultivar is one of the Whirlybird series derived

from *Tropaeolum majus*. They are dwarf, bushy annuals that grow to 10in (25cm), bearing single or semi-double flowers without spurs in a range of colours including pink, red, yellow and orange. Flowers are produced well above the foliage throughout summer into autumn.

***Tropaeolum majus* 'Empress of India'**
A compact dwarf form that grows to 9in (23cm) tall, bearing velvety flowers of deep crimson red above foliage of a dark, bluey green edged with red, from early summer until the first frost.

Brachyscome

Brachyscome iberidifolia 'Blue Haze'
A bushy annual from southern Australia with rich blue, or in other varieties, violet or white, lightly fragrant flowers produced throughout summer and into the autumn. The Greek words *brachys comus* meaning 'short hair', from which the botanical name is derived, refers to the appearance of the foliage consisting of softly hairy stems to 18in (45cm) and leaves to 4in (10cm). This popular and frequently cultivated species is grown for its attractive bushy foliage and profusely blooming daisy flowers. Native to S Australia. Hardy to 10°F (–12°C), US zones 8–10. *Brachycome iberidifolia* and its cultivars are the varieties usually grown in gardens.

PLANTING HELP   Plant in any reasonable potting mix in shelter and sun. Sow seed in March and plant seedlings outside in May, or sow seed directly outside in May.

Erigeron

Erigeron karvinskianus (syn, *Erigeron mucronatus*)   A vigorous perennial with branching stems that grow 6–12in (15–30cm) long, and hairy, grey green leaves to 1½in (4cm) long, bearing masses of yellow-centred flower heads, either singly or in small groups, in summer. The flowers begin white and become pink or purple. Truly excellent for filling out spaces in pots and for planting among paving stones and in crevices in walls along patio edges. Hardy to 20°F (–6°C), US zones 9–10. Native to Central America.

PLANTING HELP   Plant in rich compost which does not dry out in summer. Prefers full sun. Cut back in autumn. Sow seed in containers, divide or take cuttings in spring.

Felicia

Felicia amelloides Blue Daisy, Blue Marguerite
A hairy sub-shrub that grows to 24in (60cm) tall, bearing numerous light blue daisy flowers with yellow centres, which close in overcast weather. Leaves to 1¼in (3cm) long. Hardy to 32°F (0°C), US zone 10.
Felicia amoena 'Variegata' is similar in flower, but with broader white-variegated foliage. Both are native to South Africa.

PLANTING HELP   Plant in any reasonable potting compost in full sun and pinch back growing shoots to produce a bushier plant. These plants will not thrive in damp conditions. Felicias are commonly grown as annuals and grow well in summer pots and window boxes; they can be grown in a cool greenhouse or conservatory and moved outside in warm weather.

Erigeron karvinskianus is good in a pot or a crevice

Brachyscome iberidifolia 'Blue Haze' at Levens Hall

Felicia amelloides with orange, nodding *Glumicalyx gosoleiodes* at Wisley

Felicia amoena 'Variegata' at Powis Castle

Bidens ferulifolia (pointed petals) and *Tagetes tenuifolia* (blunt petals) with petunias and pelargoniums

Euryops pectinatus in a pot in Eccleston Square

Asteriscus

Asteriscus maritimus
(syn. *Asteriscus* 'Gold Coin')
A perennial that grows to 10in
(25cm) tall, bearing orange
yellow, daisy-like flowers.
Hardy to 0°F (−18°C),
US zones 7–10. Native
to the Canary Islands
and their near neighbours,
the Cape Verde Islands.

PLANTING HELP   Plant
in good, sandy compost in
full sun. Keep dry in winter.
This can be raised from seed but it
is probably better to buy a young
plant from the garden centre.

Asteriscus
maritimus

Bidens

Bidens ferulifolia   A short-lived perennial,
often grown as an annual, that grows to 12in
(30cm) tall, bearing fern-like green leaves to 3in
(8cm) long, producing daisy-like, bright yellow
flowers from midsummer to autumn. Its rambling

African marigolds are ideal for exposed dry places

French Marigolds

habit makes this a perfect specimen for hanging baskets, window boxes, planters and containers. Hardy to 20°F (–6°C), US zones 9–10. Native to southwestern USA and Mexico.

PLANTING HELP   Plant in full sun in any reasonable potting mix. Sow seed in warmth in spring. Root perennial cuttings in spring or autumn or divide perennials when growth begins in spring.

Euryops

Euryops pectinatus   An upright shrub that grows to 3¼ft (1m) tall with hairy grey leaves to 3in (8cm) long, bearing bright yellow flowers 2in (5cm) across, on long stalks throughout summer. Hardy to 32°F (0°C), US zone 10. Native to South Africa, and commonly grown outside in California.

PLANTING HELP   Plant in any reasonable potting mix in full sun. Water well during growth. Sow seed in warmth in spring.

American Marigolds

Not to be confused with the English or Pot Marigold *Calendula officinalis*, this genus of about 50 different erect, bushy, aromatic annuals and herbaceous perennials has the Latin name *Tagetes*. They are now available in brilliant shades and combinations of cream, yellow, gold and orange, and originate from hot dry slopes and valleys in southern USA, Central and South America, although there is one species which is native to Africa. Many cultivars have been developed.

Tagetes can be classified into four main groups which describe their characteristics and parentage: African, French, Afro-French and Signet. All make wonderful plants for containers, window boxes, hanging baskets and planters. Hardy to 32°F (0°C), US zone 10.

PLANTING HELP   Plant in full sun in loam-based potting compost. Water well in the growing season and apply a liquid fertilizer occasionally. Dead-head to prolong flowering. Sow seed thinly in March and plant outside in May or June.

African Marigolds   Large-flowered compact annuals derived from *T. erecta*, bearing angular, hairless stems producing leaves 2–4in (5–10cm) long made up of narrow leaflets, and producing large pompom flower heads 5in (12cm) wide, in oranges and yellows, from spring to autumn.

French Marigolds   Small-flowered compact annuals derived from *T. patula* bearing hairless, purple-tinged stems to 4in (10cm) long, made up of leaflets 1¼in (3cm) long, and producing solitary, usually double, red brown, yellow, orange or bicoloured flower heads 2in (5cm) wide, from spring to autumn.

Tagetes tenuifolia **'Golden Gem'**   This is one of the Gem series of Signet marigolds which will grow to 9in (23cm) tall. All are upright annuals bearing branching stems with leaves 2–5in (5–12cm) long , made up of leaflets ¾in (2cm) long, and producing many single, yellow, orange or red flower heads 1in (2.5cm) wide, from late spring to autumn.

57

Ice Plants, marigolds and godetias on a Cornish 'Hedge'

Gazanias with *Senecio cineraria*

Gazania 'Mini-Star' in mixed colours

Gazania seedlings in shades of brown

Mesembryanthemum

Ice Plant, Mesem *Dorotheanthus bellidiflorus* (syn. *Mesembryanthemum criniflorum*) A dwarf annual that grows to 4in (10cm) tall, bearing daisy-like flowers 3in (8cm) wide, with shiny petals in shades of yellow, pink, mauve or white, each with a dark centre. The blue green leaves are covered with transparent crystals making them look as if they are encrusted with ice. Hardy to 20°F (–6°C), US zones 9–10. Native to South Africa.

PLANTING HELP Seed can be sown in autumn in mild areas or in spring in cooler climates. Plant in any reasonable potting mix, water well in spring but less during flowering. Best in full sun.

Gazania

Gazania **'Mini-Star' mixed** Garden hybrid gazanias are derived from South African species. Although actually tender perennials, they are often treated as half-hardy annuals. They grow to 8in (20cm) tall, producing a succession of large, showy, daisy flowers in a wide range of colours, many with darker centres, in summer. The foliage is a highly ornamental silvery green. Hardy to 20°F (–6°C), US zones 9–10. Gazanias are showy plants for containers and window boxes. The flowers may close on dull days or in cool weather.

PLANTING HELP Sow seed indoors in early spring. The seedlings should be hardened off gradually and planted out after all risk of frost has passed. Plant in full sun in any reasonable, well-drained compost.

Portulaca grandiflora 'Sundial Mango'

Osteospermum caulescens in an old chimney pot

Lampranthus brownii, good in drought and full sun

Osteospermum

Osteospermum caulescens (syn. *Osteospermum ecklonis* var. *prostratum*)   A prostrate sub-shrub that grows to 4in (10cm) tall, bearing lance-shaped, toothed leaves 4in (10cm) long, and producing solitary, daisy-like flowers 2–2½in (5–6cm) across, white flushed purple with blue grey centres, from late spring to autumn. Hardy to 20°F (–6°C), US zones 9–10.

PLANTING HELP   Plant in shelter and full sun. Dead-head regularly to prolong flowering. Sow seed in warmth in spring.

Lampranthus

Lampranthus brownii   A small shrubby succulent from South Africa which flowers profusely, producing shiny blooms up to 3in (8cm) across. Very useful for pots, window boxes and hanging baskets. This plant can be grown in any zone but will be killed by the first frost.

PLANTING HELP   Plant in any standard cactus potting mix in full sun. Water moderately and feed every month or two.

Portulaca

***Portulaca grandiflora* 'Sundial Mango'**   A sprawling red-stemmed annual that grows 12in (30cm) across, bearing clusters of cylindrical, fleshy green leaves to 1in (2.5cm) long, producing double, peach-coloured flowers 1in (2.5cm) wide and slashed with scarlet in their centres. The Sundial series of cultivars was produced to provide long-flowering cultivars in poor conditions. These are truly beautiful plants for a container or window box. Hardy to 32°F (0°C), US zone 10.

PLANTING HELP   Plant in poor, sandy, well-drained compost in full sun. Sow seed in warmth in spring. Aphids can cause problems.

Chrysanthemum 'Seaton's Sulphur'

Chrysanthemum 'Yellow Spray' at Wisley

Chrysanthemum

Pot-grown dwarf chrysanthemums (syn. *Dendranthemum*) are ideal for patio, cold greenhouse or conservatory display. The so-called Charm or Cascade chrysanthemums are best for this purpose, but any short-growing sorts may be used as well. Plants grow to 1ft (30cm) tall or more if trained, bearing masses of single flowers in white, yellow, pink, red or purple in autumn. Hardy to 10°F (−12°C), US zones 8–10.

PLANTING HELP   For fertile, moist, well-drained compost in full sun. Take cuttings in late winter, and pot up young plants in spring. Charm chrysanthemums need no training or pinching; Cascades can be trained into fans, hanging shapes or almost anything.

Marguerite

Argyranthemum frutescens
(syn. *Chrysanthemum frutescens*)   Evergreen sub-shrubs native to the Canary Islands and Madeira, which make excellent container plants, as they can be trained into elegant shapes. They bear a succession of daisy flowers, each 2–2½in (5–6cm) wide, above finely divided, often bluish grey foliage, throughout the summer. Numerous hybrids are available, with flowers usually white but in a few varieties pink or pale yellow. Hardy to 20°F (−7°C), US zones 9–10, so they can be treated as shrubby perennials in mild winter areas.

PLANTING HELP
Propagate from cuttings in the summer and overwinter young plants in a greenhouse or buy plants from your local nursery. Best in a sheltered, sunny position, marguerites can be planted out in late spring and need fertile, well-drained soil.

Yellow
Marguerite

Chrysanthemum 'Bronze Arola'

CHRYSANTHEMUMS & MARGUERITES

Trained Cascade and Charm chrysanthemums in the cold greenhouse at Wisley

Shrubby marguerites among other pots in Eccleston Square

Plumbago in a large pot at Villa Pallavicino

Honeysuckle as a standard

Jasminum grandiflorum, small cuttings in a pot

Lonicera × italica, often called L. × americana

Scrambling Shrubs

Climbers come in many shapes and sizes and many can be grown in containers. Given some care and a big enough receptacle, quite large specimens can be produced, although smaller plants look extremely effective twisting among other shrubs and trees, or even trained around a pole in the centre of a pot.

Climbers require support in the form of sticks, wires, trelliswork or a stiff shrub. Remember that some plants grow faster than others and require more work in the form of pruning; rapid growers, like honeysuckle and jasmine, can soon become rather overwhelming where space is restricted and annual thinning is essential. Climbers can fulfil a variety of functions; some are valued for their foliage, others are grown for their flowers and many flowering species are chosen for scent.

Bougainvillea

Bougainvillea glabra   A vigorous climbing shrub with curved thorns that grows to about 8ft (2.5m) when grown in a pot. Small insignificant white flowers are surrounded by brilliantly coloured outer petals (bracts) in various shades of reddish purple, white, pink, yellow or orange. Hardy to 20°F (-6°C), US zones 9–10 once established, but can be brought inside to a conservatory during colder months. There are many beautiful hybrids, cultivars and mutations with single or double bracts. Native to South America.

Bougainvilleas in pots in Oaxaica, Mexico

PLANTING HELP   Plant in full sun in a mixture of loam and peat-based compost and feed with a high nitrogen fertilizer during the growing season. Be careful of roots when repotting and do not press compost down too firmly. Bougainvilleas may drop their leaves and become semi-dormant during cold weather.

Plumbago

Plumbago auriculata Cape Leadwort
An evergreen scrambling shrub that grows 10–20ft (3–6m), although it will probably not exceed 10ft (3m) when grown in a pot. It bears oblong leaves 1½–3in (4–8cm) long and produces clusters, about 6in (15cm) wide, of pale blue flowers from summer to late autumn. There is also a form with white flowers and one with flowers of slightly deeper blue. Container-grown plants will do well outside in hot summers and can be moved into a greenhouse or conservatory in cold winters. Native to South Africa. Hardy to 20°F (–6°C), US zones 9–10.

PLANTING HELP   Plant in loam-based compost in full sun and top dress or repot in spring. Water carefully and feed monthly during growing season to keep the plant flowering freely; keep dry in winter. Root cuttings in summer.

Honeysuckle

Lonicera × italica (syn. *L. × americana* hort.)
A vigorous deciduous climber that grows up to 10ft (3m) in a large pot but can grow to 30ft (9m) tall if planted in the ground. It bears pairs of oval leaves, each about 3in (8cm) long and produces clusters of fragrant, pinky yellow flowers, 2in (5cm) long, in early summer. Hardy to –10°F (–23°C), US zones 6–9.

PLANTING HELP   Plant in shade or partial shade; it is important to keep the roots cool when growing in containers. To establish a good framework and encourage branching, prune young specimens by shortening stems, then prune regularly to control growth and thin out old wood to prevent too much crowding after flowering.

Jasmines

Jasminum grandiflorum   An evergreen scrambling shrub that grows 10–20ft (3–6m), but can be kept short in a pot. The wonderfully scented flowers, around 1in (2.5cm) across, are produced in autumn and winter. Hardy to 20°F (–6°C), US zones 9–10.

PLANTING HELP   As for Plumbago.

Roses

'Lady Sunblaze'

A garden does not seem complete without roses and the container garden is no exception. Repeat-flowering Hybrid Teas, Floribundas and Patio and Miniature roses are the best choice because they provide such a dazzling display of colour over a long period and all make splendid container plants; indeed many Miniatures are so small that they can seem rather insignificant in a bed.

Most Old roses are not ideal for containers, but the English roses, raised by David Austin, will produce flowers in the old style, on healthy bushes which repeat well in late summer and autumn. Climbers and Ramblers will need very large pots to support their extensive top growth. All are hardy to −10°F (−23°C), US zones 6–9.

PRUNING & PLANTING HELP
Place a single rose in a container about 16–24in (40–60cm) wide by 16in (40cm) deep, in sun, or partial shade in hot areas. Water freely in warm weather and apply liquid feed monthly from late spring to early autumn; remember that contained roses need feeding more regularly than those in beds. Remove dead flowers with about three leaves to encourage new flowers. It is best to prune quite radically every year; shorten stems by a third in autumn or cut back to about 6–8in (15–20cm) in spring. Removing old or weak branches near the base occasionally will stimulate new growth.

Climbers and ramblers are all the better for rooting into the ground through the base of the pot. Prune by removing the shoots which have flowered and tying in the new shoots which will flower the following year.

Rose 'Gentle Touch' A free-flowering, scented Miniature or Patio rose that grows to 1ft (30cm) tall. Flowers continuously throughout summer.

Rose 'Green Ice' A free-flowering Miniature which is very good in hanging baskets. Grows to 1½ft (45cm) tall with a wonderful scent.

Rose 'Lady Sunblaze' A Miniature bearing very full flowers and small-leaved, bushy foliage.

Rose 'Nozomi' A rampant, spreading Miniature that can be grown as a weeping standard. Summer-flowering only with small, single flowers. Grows to 6ft (2m) or more across.

Rose 'Sharifa Asma' One of the most delicate of the English roses, raised by David Austin in 1989. Repeat-flowers well. Grows to 3ft (90cm) tall with wonderfully scented, pale pink fully double flowers.

Rose 'Suma' Double flowers on dense and trailing foliage, grows to 1ft (30cm) tall. Repeat-flowering. Tolerates shade. A strong scent.

Rose 'Yvonne Rabier' A very healthy repeat-flowering hybrid with very glossy leaves. Grows to 3ft (90cm) tall with a wonderful scent.

Rose 'Gentle Touch'

Roses in a mixed planting

ROSES

English Rose 'Sharifa Asma'

Rose 'Green Ice' on wooden decking in New South Wales

Polyantha 'Yvonne Rabier'

Rose 'Suma' grown as a pot standard

Rose 'Nozomi' grown in a pot

Lantana camara at Villa Pallavicino

Tender Shrubs

The advantage of growing tender shrubs in containers is that they can be enjoyed outside in the summer and, if necessary, brought into a shed, conservatory or greenhouse in the winter.

Abutilon

Abutilon × *hybridum* **'Canary Bird'**
A. × *hybridum* is a group of semi-evergreen shrubs that grows to 6ft (1.8m) tall, producing bell-shaped, pendulous flowers about 1½in (4cm) wide, with rounded petals and a central boss of stamens, over a long period in summer and early autumn. The oval leaves are about 6in (15cm) long. Hardy to 20°F (−6°C), US zones 9–10. Other colours include 'Ashford Red', 'Silver Belle' (white) and 'Nabob' (deepest crimson). The related *A. megapotamicum* and its hybrids have smaller flowers and a red calyx. Like many fast-growing shrubs, abutilons are inclined to be short-lived but look wonderful in a container on a sunny patio.

PLANTING HELP   Plant in any reasonable potting compost in early spring in full sun. For good, rich soil in full sun. Little pruning is required other than to keep a young plant to a single stem. Later, leggy plants can be reduced by a third in late winter.

Lantana

Lantana camara   A group of evergreen shrubs that grows 3–6ft (1–1.8m) high, often with prickly stems, bearing slightly toothed, crinkled green leaves 2–4in (5–10cm) long, and producing flower heads 1–2in (2.5–5cm) across in summer and autumn. Colours range from white to shades of yellow, pink, red and purple, and some cultivars exhibit more than one colour. Lantana make excellent plants for containers and can be grown as standards. Their beautiful flower heads are also attractive to butterflies. All are frost-tender, not tolerating temperatures below 41°F (5°C), the warmer parts of zone 10.

PLANTING HELP   For full sun in any reasonable potting mix. Water freely during growth, keep moist in winter and feed once a month. Sow seed in warmth in spring and root cuttings in summer.

Hibiscus

Chinese Hibiscus *Hibiscus rosa-sinensis*
An evergreen shrub thought to be native to tropical Asia, that grows to about 8ft (2.5m), bearing glossy green leaves 6in (15cm) long, and producing solitary red flowers with petals 2½–5in (6–12cm) long, from summer to autumn. There are numerous showy cultivars in a profusion of colours. The flowers of most cultivars last for only one day. Hardy to 41°F (5°C), the warmer parts of zone 10. This plant very definitely needs the protection of a conservatory in cooler climates, although it can be moved outside at the height of a warm summer when night temperatures exceed 75°F (25°C). It is worth remembering that the length of the flowering season and the pigmentation of individual blooms can be affected by extremes of temperature. The East African *H. schizopetalus* (*not illustrated*) has nodding flowers with deeply cut petals and a very long bunch of styles and stamens.

PLANTING HELP   Plant in autumn or spring in well-drained compost in sun and shelter or in a cool greenhouse or conservatory. Do not be discouraged if many of the leaves drop off in the winter; keep the plants dry and in the spring they will regenerate. Prune out old wood in spring to encourage new growth.

Oleander

Nerium oleander   Evergreen shrubs or small trees that grow to 25ft (8m) with narrow leaves, usually in whorls of 3. Flowers in loose heads, pink

TENDER SHRUBS

An oleander, the old variety 'Splendens', in the ruins of Pompeii

or reddish, white or pale orange or yellow, 1–2in (2.5–5cm) across, from April to September. Hardy to 20°F (–6°C), US zones 9–10.
'Splendens' An old variety that is still commonly grown, with large, double, rich pink flowers. There is a variegated form of this with yellow-edged leaves.

PLANTING HELP Oleanders need full sun. They are planted everywhere in subtropical areas and are good in pots brought indoors in winter in frosty climates. They are heat- and drought-resistant once established, but need ample water in summer if grown in pots. All parts of the plant are very poisonous.

Nerium oleander

Abutilon 'Canary Bird'

Chinese Hibiscus *Hibiscus rosa-sinensis*

Brugmansia arborea at Herrenhausen, Hanover, northern Germany

Angels' Trumpets

There are about 5 species and many hybrids of *Brugmansia*, sometimes still called by the old name of *Datura*; all are evergreen shrubs or small trees, producing huge single, usually fragrant, bell-shaped flowers from spring to autumn. They grow 6–30ft (2–10m) but may easily be kept to 7ft (2m) in large pots.

PLANTING HELP   Place in full sun or partial shade and shelter from wind. Give ample water in summer, keep drier in winter. Heavy feeding and ample water with liquid fertilizer will produce large, lush leaves and plenty of flowers. Be sure to bring under cover before the first frost.

Brugmansia arborea (syn. *Datura cornigera*) A shrub that grows to 12ft (4m) tall, bearing fragrant, funnel-shaped, nodding white flowers, 5–6in (12–15cm), from late spring to summer. Native to South America. Hardy to 41°F (5°C), the warmer parts of US zone 10.

***Brugmansia* × *candida* 'Grand Marnier'** A fine hybrid with soft, apricot yellow, scented flowers which open pale yellow.

Brugmansia 'Grand Marnier'

Brugmansia × *insignis* grown in a pot in Devon

A lacecap hydrangea in a half barrel

Brugmansia × insignis An easily grown hybrid for a large pot, with pinkish flowers which open wide in the evening.

Hydrangea

Hydrangeas are deciduous or evergreen shrubs and climbers from the woods of Asia and America, grown primarily for their magnificent flower heads, either mophead or lacecap. The flower colour of *H. macrophylla* is affected by the alkalinity of the soil; acid soils produce blue flowers, whereas neutral to alkaline soils produce pink flowers. It is possible to introduce a blueing agent, such as aluminium sulphate, to the compost if it is neutral. However, there are white-flowered varieties whose colour is unaffected by the pH of the soil.

PLANTING HELP Ensure that blue-flowered varieties are planted in ericaceous compost and put lots of pebbles in the bottom of the container. Further applications of aluminium sulphate, sold as hydrangea colourant, may be needed to keep the flowers blue, and rainwater or cold tea should be used in areas where the tap water is alkaline. The plants should be potted up in winter and kept cold for flowering in summer. Alternatively, plants which have been brought into flower in winter, in a heated greenhouse, may be bought as houseplants.

Common Hydrangea *Hydrangea macrophylla* A deciduous shrub that can be grown to flower in winter, producing plants with a profusion of blooms and less foliage. It grows to 4ft (1.2m) tall, bearing glossy green leaves to 8in (20cm) long and producing flower heads 6–8in (15–20cm) wide. These make excellent houseplants. Native to Japan. Hardy to –20°F (–29°C), US zones 5–9. There are many cultivars, with both mophead and lacecap flower heads, varying in height from 3–6ft (90–180cm), flowering normally in late summer. All varieties will do well in pots, provided they have ample water while in growth, and pot culture has the advantage that the plants can be brought under cover if a late frost is threatened.

Lacecap hydrangea 'Snow'

69

Fuchsia

Fuchsias are ideal plants for containers. Their dainty flowers are distinctive, with their thick recurving sepals, cups of overlapping petals and protruding styles. Fuchsias remain in flower over a long period in summer and grow well in containers, window boxes and hanging baskets, provided they get sufficient water and fertilizer.

Those with sturdy erect stems can make large shrubs and may be trained as standards or bushes, although it is possible to shape them into fans or pyramids too. They make a perfect centrepiece for a large, mixed container but also look attractive when planted alone. To produce a successful standard, stake the stem when planting by placing a cane next to the plant and removing any side shoots until the desired height is reached. Remember to tie up the stem as it grows and then remove the growing points to make the plant branch, allowing 5 or 6 strong shoots to develop into the head. It is possible to grow trailing fuchsias as weeping standards but they are easier to grow in window boxes and hanging baskets; pinching out the growing point will produce a bushier plant, although this should not be done before the plant has produced three sets of leaves.

Most of the varieties used for pots, including those illustrated, are frost-tender, generally to 32°F (0°C), US zone 10 or slightly less for a short time.

PLANTING HELP Wild fuchsias are plants of mountain forest and all fuchsias need moist, well-drained compost in sun or partial shade and shelter. Keep potted plants frost-free and rather dry in winter. Water well during growth and fertilize weekly with a liquid feed. Mist foliage in hot weather to increase humidity and remove dead flowers. Root softwood cuttings in spring or semi-ripe cuttings in late summer.

Fuchsia fulgens
A shrub that can grow to 4ft (1.2m), but usually about 15in (40cm), producing very narrow flowers 2½–4in (6–10cm) long, with a dull scarlet or orange tube, sepals yellow or red at the base, with green tips and scarlet petals. Native to Mexico. Easily grown and free-flowering in warm, sunny, humid conditions and rich well-drained soil. Can be left dry and leafless in winter.

Fuchsia fulgens

Fuchsia 'Orient Express' and 'Loxensis'
These long-tubed hybrids are hybrids of *F. fulgens*. They are generally less hardy than the usual short-tubed fuchsias and prefer moist, humid and shady conditions in summer. They need protection from all frost in winter.

Fuchsia 'Loxensis' at Levens Hall

Fuchsia 'Orient Express' with *Phormium* 'Sundowner'

Standard fuchsia in a pot in Eccleston Square

Fuchsia 'Carmel Blue' at Herrenhausen, near Hanover

Fuchsia 'Carmel Blue' An old cultivar, dating from 1956. Single flowers with white sepals and blue petals. Very free-flowering.

Fuchsia 'Celia Smedley' Vigorous bushy growth up to 30in (75cm). Medium-sized single flowers, freely borne. Tube and sepals rose pink, petals red. Responds well to pinching back. Roots easily.

Fuchsia 'Checkerboard' A free-flowering variety, and one of the best for a hanging basket. Medium-sized flowers have red tubes, red outer sepals with white tips and dark red petals.

Fuchsia 'Eleanor Leytham' Upright bushy compact growth. Small flowers freely produced. Tube and sepals white, flushed with pink; petals edged with deep pink.

Fuchsia 'Lord Lonsdale' Bushy but lax. Medium-sized single flowers. Tube and sepals apricot; petals orangey apricot. Often confused with 'Aurora Superba', but has lighter green foliage and petals are larger and lighter in colour.

Fuchsia 'Jomam' Upright bushy growth, quite small. Medium-sized single flowers with rose pink tube and sepals and pale violet petals, lightly

veined with pink. Does well in cool conditions, away from direct sunlight.

Fuchsia 'Florabelle' A variety with masses of flowers on a tidy plant that grows 14in (35cm) tall.

Fuchsia 'Linda Goulding' Upright bushy growth. Medium-sized single flowers. Short white tube, reflexed pink sepals; petals white with pale pink veining.

Fuchsia 'Pink Fantasia' A bushy plant with masses of single flowers held erect. Tube and sepals pink, petals purple, shading to dark purple edges.

Fuchsia 'Ruddigore'
A bushy plant with single flowers. Long tube and sepals salmon orange; petals bright orange.

Fuchsia 'Checkerboard'

FUCHSIAS

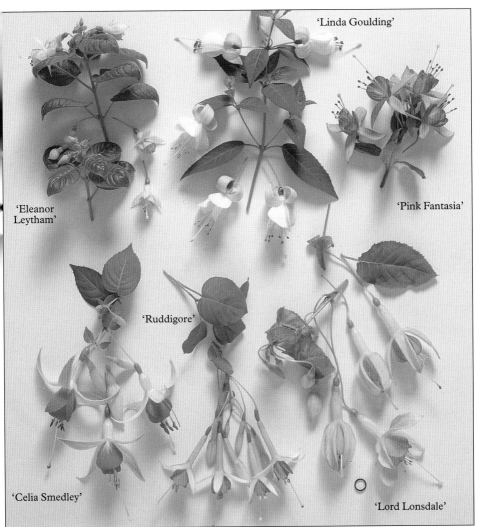

'Linda Goulding'

'Eleanor
Leytham'

'Pink Fantasia'

'Ruddigore'

'Celia Smedley'

'Lord Lonsdale'

Specimens from Oldbury Nurseries, Bethersden, Kent, ⅓ life-size

Fuchsia 'Florabelle' in a hanging basket

Fuchsia 'Jomam'

Begonia tuberosa 'Pin Up'

Pendula begonia 'Ophelia'

Begonia

The name *Begonia* commemorates Michel Bégon (1638–1710), a French governor of Canada and an enthusiastic patron of botany. Begonias are sub-shrubs or perennials from all the tropical areas of the world. There are two main types which have been developed in gardens: those with fibrous roots and those which grow from tubers, and there is a vast range of cultivars of both types now available from garden centres. Many will withstand quite dense shade, and there are varieties with richly coloured foliage and attractive blooms. It is well worth the effort involved in growing them as they look wonderful in pots, containers and window boxes, and pendulous cultivars make excellent hanging-basket plants. They can be grown in any zone but will not withstand frost.

Tuberous Begonias   Considered by many to epitomize the very best of bedding plants, these provide a dazzling variety of colour right through until the first frosts. They are perennials derived from South American species, pendant or upright with sparsely branched stems and glossy green, pointed leaves. Most bear clusters of double flowers in summer and remain dormant in winter.

Begonia tuberosa **'Pin Up'**   A single-flowered strain which can be raised from seed to flower the same year. Flowers 4–5in (10–12cm) wide, white with a pink frilly edge.

Begonia tuberosa **'Illumination'**   One of the Illumination series of pendulous begonias that grows to 24in (60cm) tall, bearing oval green leaves to 7in (18cm) long, producing cascades of double flowers 3in (8cm) across, in summer.

PLANTING HELP   Tuberous begonias are usually bought as dormant tubers in spring. They should be started into growth in heat, and then planted either in large pots or hanging baskets, then put outside when all danger of frost is past, and the weather has warmed up. Tuberous begonias do best in the shade in areas with hot summers, or in partial sun in areas with cool summers, such as the coast of California or the extreme west of Europe. They do best in peaty or leafy soil with good drainage, but ample water in hot weather. Modern varieties, such as the 'Pin Up' strain can be grown from seed sown in warmth in early spring.

Tuberous begonias in Eccleston Square

Begonias and impatiens in pots around a fountain at Chewton Glen, Hampshire

Tuberous begonias with *Lantana montevidensis* in a shallow urn

Semperflorens Begonias

These are fibrous rooted, compact, bushy evergreen perennials with attractive flowers and foliage. They are derived from the Brazilian *Begonia semperflorens* which reaches 18in (45cm) in the wild. However, a great deal of effort has gone into reducing the size of the plant, increasing the colour range of the flowers and developing the dark-leaved varieties now available as cultivars; the emphasis has been to produce an abundance of smaller flowers, rather than a few large blooms. The leaves are rounded, 1¼–4in (3–10cm) long, and the single or double flowers ½–1in (1–2.5cm) wide, are produced in summer. Hardy to 32°F (0°C), US zone 10 or slightly less for a short time.

Begonia semperflorens **'Cocktail Series'**
A series of mixed colours, characterized by their purplish leaves and ability to stand rain and wind in summer.

Begonia semperflorens **'Victory White'**
One of the Victory series of begonias that grows to 10in (25cm) tall, bearing rounded leaves and single flowers to 1½in (4cm) across in summer.

Begonia semperflorens **'Olympia Light Pink'**
One of the Olympic series of compact, weather-resistant plants that grows to 8in (20cm) tall, with rounded leaves and pale pink flowers 1½in (4cm) across in summer.

PLANTING HELP   The Semperflorens varieties can be grown from seed or from young plants purchased from a nursery. Seed should be sown indoors at 60°F (15°C) in January and lightly covered in a seed compost containing some sand and kept moist. The seedlings should be hardened off gradually and planted out after all risk of frost has passed. Young plants will grow best in humus-rich compost in partial shade.

Elatior Begonias

Begonia **'Elatior Group'**   These are compact, double-flowered begonias, in a wide range of colours bred from winter-flowering begonias for the potted plant trade, to flower from late summer to winter. They are easily grown and flower for a long period.

PLANTING HELP   The 'Elatior Group' is generally bought in flower, but may be propagated by cuttings in the spring.

Begonia semperflorens in a range of colours including the purple-leaved 'Cocktail Series'

SEMPERFLORENS BEGONIAS

Begonia semperflorens 'Victory White' with verbena and gazanias

Begonia semperflorens 'Olympia Light Pink' with
Scaevola 'Blue Fan'

Elatior group begonias used for bedding

Late-flowering Bulbs

Bulbs and tubers are extremely useful container plants, producing leaves and flowers in a relatively short time and mixing well with shrubs and perennials. Summer-flowering bulbs are planted in the spring. They can provide a wonderful display when in bloom and are useful in that they can be planted under other plants, ready to revive the appearance of a container when the other inhabitants have finished flowering.

Cyclamen

Cyclamen persicum hybrids   Grows to 8in (20cm) tall, bearing heart-shaped leaves 1–5in (2.5–12cm) long, dark green often speckled with silver, and producing scented pink, red or white flowers ¾in (2cm) long, which stand well above the leaves, from early winter to early spring. Native to SE Mediterranean and N Africa. There are many cultivars varying from 6–12in (15–30cm) tall, in an abundance of reds, pinks, whites and purples. Hardy to 20°F (–6°C), US zones 9–10.

PLANTING HELP   Plant with the tops of the tubers just visible in loam-based potting compost in bright light, in reasonable humidity in a draught-free site. Water less after flowering and keep dry when dormant. These cyclamens grow best in a cool greenhouse and adapt very well to use as a houseplant.

Lilium 'Stargazer' with petunias in a fine blue pot

Large-flowered *Cyclamen persicum*

Lilium regale

Meadow Saffron with *Liriope muscari*

Lilies

Lilies are among the best bulbs for pots, providing spectacular flowers in summer.

PLANTING HELP   Lilies need fairly deep containers and reasonable, well-drained compost. Pot bulbs in spring in a sheltered position, covering the compost with a layer of peat or leaf mould to allow roots to develop, before moving into their summer positions. Propagate by division of the clumps, removing offsets during the dormant period.

Regal Lily *Lilium regale*   This species from W China quickly became amazingly popular in the West when it was introduced to the Arnold Arboretum in Massachusetts. It is a vigorous stem-rooting lily that grows to 4ft (1.2m) tall, with erect or arching stems and leaves 2–5in (5–12cm) long, producing clusters of trumpet-shaped white flowers 5–6in (12–15cm) long, flushed brownish red outside and yellow with gold anthers inside, in summer. A well-established plant will produce as many as 15 large, trumpet-shaped flowers. Hardy to 10°F (−12°C), US zones 8–10. Native to north-western China. Needs very well-drained, limy soil beneath the bulbs.

Lilium **'Butter Pixie'**   Excellent for pot culture and for flowering in the house. The colours are vibrant and true. Grows 12–15in (30–40cm).

Lilium **'Orange Pixie'**   Excellent for pot culture and for flowering in the house. The colours are vibrant and true. Grows 12–15in (30–40cm).

Lilium **'Stargazer'**   An Oriental hybrid that produces red flowers with white borders and upright habit to 3ft (90cm) tall, from July to August. A good plant for a large pot with superbly scented flowers which last well. Best in acid, sandy soil.

Small-flowered *Cyclamen persicum*

Lily 'Butter Pixie' and 'Orange Pixie'

Meadow Saffron

Colchicum autumnale Meadow Saffron
An upright plant that grows 4–6in (10–15cm) tall which produces 1–6 crocus-like pink flowers in the autumn, followed in spring by broad, shiny green leaves. Hardy to 10°F (−12°C), US zones 8–10.

PLANTING HELP   Plant in late summer. Set corms 2–3in (5–8cm) apart in sun. Divide clumps while dormant in summer. During growing period, water regularly and in mass-planted containers apply liquid feed every 10–14 days.

Hippeastrum vittatum in a garden in western China

Hippeastrum 'Apple Blossom'

Nerine

A genus of around 30 species, native to South Africa. The flowering stems carry an umbel of flowers with narrow, wavy-edged petals, followed by round, fleshy seeds. Varieties are now available with flowers in all shades of pink, scarlet, salmon and white.

Nerine bowdenii A summer-growing bulb with green shiny leaves and upright umbels of pale pink flowers, native to the summer-rainfall area of South Africa, flowering in autumn. Leaves to 1ft (30cm) long, appearing in spring. Hardy to 20°F (–6°C), US zones 9–10.

Nerine sarniensis A winter-growing bulb with greyish leaves and upright umbels of bright scarlet flowers with a golden sheen, native to the Cape area of South Africa, flowering in autumn. Leaves to 1ft (30cm) long, appearing with or shortly after the flowers. Keep dry in summer, but with monthly waterings to promote flowering. Hardy to 32°F (0°C), US zone 10.

Nerine 'Zeal Giant' A hybrid of *Nerine bowdenii*, possibly with a *Brunsvigia*. Long, deep pink flowers. Hardy to 20°F (–6°C), US zones 9–10. Nerine hybrids have been developed over many years, but have never achieved great popularity as they are slow to propagate in large numbers and therefore expensive; however, they do look wonderful in pots. The 1980s and 90s produced further improvements; the aim has been to widen the colour range and the flowering season and produce larger, longer-lasting flowers.

Nerine 'Zeal Giant' at Marwood Hill, Devon

Nerine sarniensis, a very old group crowded into a large pot

Nerine bowdenii with *Liriope muscari* in Sussex

PLANTING HELP   For stony compost and a warm position. The pots of tender species do well stood outside in summer and flower before the leaves in early autumn.

Hippeastrum

A genus of bulbs native to diverse habitats in Central and South America. The flowering stems carry an umbel of wonderfully showy, funnel-shaped flowers. Many large-flowered cultivars, commonly called *Amaryllis* have been bred for cultivation in containers. They can be grown as houseplants in winter.

Hippeastrum **'Apple Blossom'**   Grows 12–20in (30–50cm) tall, bearing pinkish flowers 4–6in (10–15cm) wide. Hardy to 32°F (0°C), US zone 10.

Hippeastrum vittatum St Joseph's Lily Grows to 3ft (90cm) tall, bearing clusters of 3–6 funnel-shaped, red-striped, white flowers 5in (12cm) wide, in summer. The leaves are 24in (60cm) long. Hardy to 32°F (0°C), US zone 10.

PLANTING HELP   Plant in sandy, leafy compost, dry in winter, moist in summer. Feed fortnightly when in growth. These plants do not like root disturbance.

Canna

Canna **'Marvel'**   Canna hybrids are easily grown in pots, producing fine, broad, bright green or purple leaves and heads of colourful red, orange or yellow flowers in summer. Vary from 10ft (3m) in *C. iridiflora*, to 20in (50cm) in modern dwarf cultivars. Hardy to 32°F (0°C), US zone 10.

PLANTING HELP   Plant tubers in the spring in rich soil in a warm position. Water well while in growth and feed regularly. Lift and keep dry and frost-free in winter and spring, replant when the new growth appears.

Canna 'Marvel'

81

Mixed Foliage

It is possible to achieve truly stunning results if foliage plants are chosen with care, combining different types of foliage which have similar horticultural needs in the same large pot or in an arrangement of smaller pots.

Hosta

Hostas are perennials that form clumps of broad, striking foliage in a diversity of sizes, shapes, textures and colours. They are easy to grow and look wonderful in pots, either on their own or as centre pieces mixed with other plants. They are not bothered by insects but slugs and snails may eat the leaves; the Japanese expect the leaves to be eaten but many Westerners prefer to protect their plants with slug pellets. We recommend using strategically placed containers of beer, which attract and then drown the enemy! Hostas are at their best in late spring, and remain attractive throughout summer, until they brighten up the dreary, late-autumn garden with creams and yellows. Hardy to −40°F (−40°C), US zones 3–8.

PLANTING HELP   Plant in early spring or late summer in fertile compost and cover with compost mixed with fine leaf mould. The hosta must be thoroughly watered-in, using a hose trickling over the hole for several hours after planting. They do well in dense or partial shade. Regular fertilizing or feeding is beneficial and will be reflected in the healthy appearance of the plant.

Hosta **'Green Fountain'**   A perennial that grows to 18in (45cm) tall, bearing lance-shaped green leaves to 10in (25cm) long, and producing funnel-shaped purple flowers 24in (60cm) long, in summer.

Hosta fortunei **var. *aureomarginata***
This plant grows to 14in (35cm) tall and 2ft (60cm) wide, bearing dark green leaves with distinct, wide golden edges and violet flowers in midsummer. Shade to three-quarters sun.

Lady's Mantle

Alchemilla mollis   The name *Alchemilla* is derived from the Arabic *alchimia* meaning 'alchemy' and originated from alchemists' belief that the plant has numerous wonder-working properties. *A mollis* is an herbaceous perennial that grows to 18in (45cm) tall, producing airy sprays of tiny yellow flowers held well above the foliage in

Hosta 'Green Fountain'

Hosta fortunei var. *aureomarginata*

Lady's Mantle *Alchemilla mollis*

summer. The softly hairy, grey green leaves are rounded, up to 6in (15cm) long. Hardy to –10°F (–23°C), US zones 6–9. This plant is seen at its best after a shower when the hairs of the foliage trap many glistening raindrops.

PLANTING HELP   Plant in autumn or early spring in any soil in sun or partial shade. Cut off the flower heads as they start to turn brown, unless you want some seedlings. This plant is quite drought-tolerant.

Ferns

Ferns are easy to grow and are available in many shades of green; some have yellow, brown or even pink new leaves. Their stately appearance introduces an element of cool freshness to the summer garden. Many ferns are also evergreen and so provide interest in winter as well. Hanging baskets bursting with ferns are truly delightful, although it is important to keep them watered, even in winter.

Common Polypody *Polypodium vulgare* in July

PLANTING HELP   Plant in a standard potting mix, water freely in summer and winter and feed weekly in spring and summer. It is important not to let the compost dry out and spraying fronds with water will pay dividends. Repot at least every three years. Ferns are primitive plants, reproducing by spores, but propagation by division is usually easy.

Soft Shield Fern *Polystichum setiferum*   A hardy and easily grown evergreen fern that grows to 4ft (1.2m) tall. The young unfurling croziers have dense, often silvery scales. Many variations in frond shape have been found. Prefers light shade. Hardy to 0°F (–18°C), US zones 7–10. Native to N Europe with similar species in both Asia and North America.

Common Polypody *Polypodium vulgare*
An evergreen fern that grows to 1ft (30cm) tall, with thin, densely packed leathery fronds, 16in (40cm) long, which will thrive in gritty compost in cool shade. Hardy to –40°F (–40°C), US zones 3–8. Native to Europe, Africa and Asia.

Soft Shield Fern *Polystichum setiferum*

Maidenhair Fern *Adiantum capillus-veneris*
A lovely evergreen fern for moist shade and shelter, especially by a pool. Often grown as a houseplant but can be grown outside in warm areas. Shiny, wiry stems with delicate leaflets up to 1ft (30cm) long. Hardy to 32°F (0°C), US zone 10. Native to many tropical and temperate regions, including the extreme west of the British Isles where there is no frost.

Maidenhair Fern *Adiantum capillus-veneris*

Agave americana with Trachycarpus in a boxwood parterre at Het Loo, Holland

Phormium 'Sundowner'

Ivy

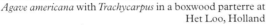

Common Ivy, English Ivy *Hedera helix* 'Ivalace'
An evergreen woody-stemmed trailing or self-clinging shrub with glossy leaves, usually less than 6in (15cm) long. Creeping or climbing to as much as 100ft (30m) tall when grown in the ground, plants will remain smaller when planted in a pot but can become shrubby with age, with less lobed leaves. Hardy to −20°F (−29°C), US zones 5–9. Native to most of Europe except the far north, east to Turkey and the Caucasus. Cultivars with green leaves are quite happy in shade, whereas variegated ivies need sun and shelter to retain their dual colouring. The many smaller cultivars of *Hedera helix* are invaluable in containers, window boxes and hanging baskets; there are several small-leaved forms and a variety of colours and shapes available.

PLANTING HELP   Plant in any reasonable potting mix, keep moist throughout the year and feed monthly during summer; mulch in autumn and spring and fertilize in spring for the best results. Some varieties may look dead after a particularly harsh winter but will recover in spring. Propagate by cuttings or by layering in summer. Water freely in summer. Insects and leaf spot may cause problems.

Phormium

Phormium 'Sundowner'   A spectacular clump-forming perennial for a container that grows to 6ft (1.8m) tall with erect evergreen, broad, bronze green leaves edged with pink, to 5ft (1.5m) long. Other varieties have pink, yellow-striped or dark green leaves, sometimes stiffly upright, sometimes arching over. Hardy to 20°F (−6°C), US zones 9–10.

PLANTING HELP   Place in fertile, moist, well-drained compost in full sun. Protect from frost. Divide in spring.

Variegated ivy with a *Podocarpus* hedge in the Harry P. Leu Gardens in Florida

Agave americana 'Marginata' with *Jasminum mesnyi* and cypresses at the hotel Reina Victoria in Ronda

Century Plant

Agave americana A perennial plant which, although it can live for up to 40 years, will die after flowering and fruiting. Grows to 6ft (1.8m) tall with serrated, lance-shaped, greyish green leaves. The flowers are yellowish green, to 4in (10cm) in length, produced in clusters up to 25ft (8m) long. Native to Mexico. **'Marginata'** has leaves with yellow margins which fade to white.

PLANTING HELP Plant agaves in standard cactus compost and place them in their containers in good light. Agaves are succulents and are able to withstand drought by storing water in their leaves for long periods. Keep the plants dry in winter, but water them freely in summer and fertilize every 4–6 weeks. Sow seed at 70°F (21°C) in spring and remove the offsets in spring or autumn and insert, unrooted, in a mixture of peat and sand, until they are rooted.

Grey foliage

Foliage is an essential part of any garden. It is the background colour on which to place the outlines of the flowers. It can enhance or detract from the overall effect of plant groupings and needs as much thought and attention as any part of the container garden.

Silver or grey foliage deserves particular attention because its ability to lift and highlight annuals and perennials is unique. Rather like painting on a white background, planting amongst grey foliage can produce spectacular results and even planted alone the variety of shapes and sizes can look stylish and elegant. All grey-leaved plants need very good drainage and should be kept rather dry through the winter.

Plecostachys serpyllifolia

Catmint

A genus of about 250 herbaceous perennials and annuals from diverse habitats in the Northern Hemisphere, hot and dry as well as cool and wet. Some *Nepeta* used to be valued for their remedial properties and they are extremely popular with cats who love to roll amongst the aromatic grey green leaves. Clusters of small tubular flowers are borne along the lengths of the upright stalks and the bushy plants remain in flower from late spring until early autumn. Dwarf varieties are perfect for containers, window boxes and hanging baskets.

PLANTING HELP For full sun or partial shade in any reasonable, well-drained potting mix. Catmint will not tolerate waterlogging, especially in the winter and a raised bed or container is ideal in this respect. If possible, trim the plants thoroughly after flowering, to encourage a second flush later in the season, and to prevent the plants from becoming too sprawling. Cuttings usually do well, and should ideally be taken from the non-flowering young shoot tips during early summer. As with other cuttings, simply trim off the lower leaves, dip in rooting hormone if you wish, and push them into a good compost of peat, sand and/or grit and keep them in a frost-free place for the winter.

Grey foliage at Hestercombe showing Lamb's Ears, yuccas, lavender and *Helichrysum* in the pot

***Nepeta glechoma* 'Variegata'** (syn. *Glechoma hederacea* 'Variegata') Variegated Ground Ivy
An evergreen trailing perennial which bears lilac flowers in summer. Hardy to –10°F (–23°C), US zones 6–9.

Nepeta* × *faasenii A low-growing perennial that grows to 1ft (30cm) tall, bearing silver leaves and producing clusters of spotted lavender flowers throughout summer. Hardy to –10°F (–23°C), US zones 6–9.

Nepeta glechoma
'Variegata'

Lamb's Ears

Stachys byzantina Grown for its attractive woolly foliage. Grows to 18in (45cm) tall with leaves 4cm (10cm) long and bearing tiny pink flowers from June to September. Native to N Turkey, N Iran and the southern Caucasus. Hardy to –20°F (–29°C), US zones 5–9.

PLANTING HELP Best in well-drained compost in full sun, protected from excessive wet in winter. Divide in spring or take cuttings in early summer. Hardy to 0°F (–18°C), US zones 7–10.

Catmint *Nepeta* × *faasenii* is good by a path

Helichrysum

Some varieties of helichrysum are grown for their foliage and are particularly attractive trailing down the sides of pots and containers.

PLANTING HELP Plant in any reasonable, slightly alkaline potting mix in full sun. Divide clumps in winter. Sow seed in containers in spring or root cuttings in summer.

Plecostachys serpyllifolia (syn. *Helichrysum microphyllum*) A straggling aromatic shrub that grows to 5ft (1.5m) tall, with stiff white stems and tiny leaves bearing clusters of diminuitive white flowers in winter and spring. Native to South Africa. Hardy to 20°F (–6°C), US zones 9–10.

Helichrysum petiolare (syn. *H. petiolatum*) An evergreen shrub providing an abundance of densely branched, soft grey foliage to almost 2ft (60cm) tall. The heart-shaped leaves are about 1½in (4cm) long and small yellow flowers are produced in late winter. There are several cultivars including a variegated form ***Helichrysum petiolare* 'Variegatum'** which has leaves marked with cream. Both are native to South Africa. Hardy to 32°F (0°C), US zone 10.

Helichrysum petiolare 'Variegatum' with lobelia

Helichrysum petiolare

Helichrysum with *Bidens* in a hanging basket

Lotus berthelotii in a strawberry pot on a pillar

***Artemisia* 'Powis Castle'** A shrubby perennial that grows to 2½ft (75cm) tall and more across, forming compact rounded clumps, providing elegant additions to larger pots and planters. Prune, if necessary, in spring only. Hardy to 10°F (–12°C), US zones 8–10.

***Artemisia absinthium* 'Lambrook Silver'** Absinth An aromatic herbaceous perennial bearing erect stems that grow to 2½ft (75cm) tall and producing silver leaves to 4in (10cm) long. Hardy to –30°F(–35°C), US zones 4–8.

Sage

Common Sage *Salvia officinalis* An aromatic, evergreen shrub native to the Mediterranean, valuable for its culinary properties as well as its attractive grey foliage. The flowering stems grow 2–3ft (60–90cm) tall and bear violet, purple pink or white flowers from mid- to late summer. Hardy to 0°F (–18°C), US zones 7–10.

PLANTING HELP For any reasonable potting mix in full sun. Keep well watered during growing season. Divide in spring. Root softwood cuttings in spring or semi-ripe cuttings in late summer.

Lotus

Lotus berthelotii This makes a wonderfully decorative container plant because of its long trailing stems, and is perfect for a tall pot, window box or hanging basket. It is a silvery sub-shrub with bright red and black flowers 1in (2.5cm) long, in spring and early summer. Cascading stems to 3½ft (1m); the leaflets fold up at night. Hardy to 32°F (0°C), US zone 10. Native to the Canary Islands and the Cape Verde Islands.

PLANTING HELP Plant in full sun in well-drained, moisture-retentive soil and protect from excess wet in winter. Easily propagated from cuttings in summer.

Artemisia

Artemisia are valued for their grey and silver, usually aromatic leaves. Some are evergreen shrubs or perennials, other herbaceous perennials, which die to the ground every winter.

PLANTING HELP Plant in any reasonable potting mix in full sun. Divide in spring and root greenwood cuttings in late spring or early summer. 'Powis Castle' can be rather slow to root. To prune, cut herbaceous perennials back to soil level in winter.

Santolina

Cotton Lavender *Santolina chamaecyparissus* A compact, slow-growing evergreen shrub that grows to 2ft (60cm) tall, with tiny yellow flowers borne in button-like flower heads ¾in (2cm) wide, on long stalks in summer, and attractive, aromatic foliage comprising hairy silver leaves, 1½in (4cm) long. Native to the Mediterranean region. Hardy to 0°F (–18°C), US zones 7–10.

PLANTING HELP Plant in any reasonable potting compost in full sun. Sow seed in containers in autumn or spring, cuttings will root best if taken in warm weather in late summer. Prune in winter, to keep tidy.

Common Sage *Salvia officinalis* along a path

GREY FOLIAGE

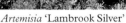

Artemisia 'Lambrook Silver'　　　　Cotton Lavender on a wall at Hestercombe

Artemisia, Melianthus, Argyranthemum, Centaurea cineraria with dissected leaves, *Teucrium* and *Rhodanthemum hosmariense* in a tour-de-force at Kiftsgate Court, Gloucestershire

Trees

As a general rule, trees planted in pots will remain small, although they do need regular feeding during growth and must not be allowed to dry out. Versailles cases, dating back to the development of the gardens of the royal estate near Paris in the 17th century, make both practical and attractive containers for trees and large shrubs; their sides can be removed, allowing old compost to be replaced and roots to be cut back a little, with minimum disturbance to the plant itself.

Citrus limon
'Quatre Saisons'

Citrus

Evergreen trees which bear clusters of waxy, scented, white flowers 1–2in (2.5–5cm) across for a long period from winter to spring. Their aromatic foliage, fragrant flowers and brightly coloured fruit combine to make them well worth growing. Indeed, the Victorians designed orangeries and orchard houses specifically to house fruit trees in tubs; these were placed outdoors in summer but were carried inside under glass in winter. Young trees take one or two years to fruit; most blossom in winter and spring.

PLANTING HELP   Buy a good plant from a reputable nursery; citrus trees can be grown from seed, but will take many years to flower and do not always come true to type. All citrus species will need protection during winter in cool climates. Plant in well-drained neutral to slightly acid

compost in full sun and water freely when in growth.

Common Lemon *Citrus limon*   A spiny, small tree that grows to 24ft (7m) tall, bearing leaves which are flushed red when young and producing scented, white flowers which are tinged purple underneath. Oval fruit to 6in (15cm) long, yellow when ripe. Introduced to the Mediterranean in the 13th century. Hardy to 20°F (–6°C), US zones 9–10 for short periods.

Potted exotic trees outside the orangery in summer at Versailles

Dwarf Peach 'Bonanza' at Reads Nursery

Peach

Prunus persica Peach 'Bonanza' A dwarf deciduous tree raised in California and particularly suitable for growing in pots indoors. These are sold budded as short standards; the shoots grow 4–6in (10–15cm) each year but are crowded with leaves, flower buds and potential fruit. They are lovely in flower and the fruit has good flavour as well. Hardy to 10°F (–12°C), US zones 8–10.

PLANTING HELP   Plant in fertile, well-drained compost in full sun. When grown or wintered indoors the leaves do not suffer from peach leaf curl, but they are susceptible to red spider mite in hot weather and care must be taken that the pots do not dry out while they are carrying fruit. Hand-pollination may be needed.

Seville Orange *Citrus aurantium* A small tree that grows to 33ft (10m) bearing leaves to 4in (10cm) long, and producing large, white, fragrant flowers, either solitary or in groups. Thick-skinned orange fruit, 2–3in (5–8cm) wide, with numerous seeds. Native to SE Asia and cultivated in Spain for its sour fruit, which is used in marmalade-making. Hardy to 32°F (0°C), US zone 10 or slightly lower for short periods.

Acer

Red Laceleaf Japanese Maple *Acer palmatum* 'Dissectum Atropurpureum' A mushroom-shaped or rounded deciduous shrub which grows slowly to 5ft (1.5m) tall. The branches are slightly arching or drooping, giving a spread a little greater than the height. The small purple flowers are rarely seen except on old bushes. In autumn the reddish purple, rounded leaves turn to shades of orange and red. Hardy to –20°F (–29°C), US zones 5–9.

PLANTING HELP   Best planted in autumn or winter, although small container-grown plants can be put in at other times of the year, if the weather is cool and damp. For a moist, acid compost that is never too dry. Place in a sheltered position in partial shade, or full sun in cool areas. Prune to reshape and remove old wood.

Seville oranges at the Villa Gamberaia, Florence

A Red Laceleaf Japanese maple

91

Potted palms *Chamaedorea elegans* in Mexico

Box topiary

Bay

Bay Tree *Laurus nobilis*   An evergreen tree that can grow to 40ft (12m) in the wild but will usually reach about 5ft (1.5m) when grown in a container. The dark green, lance-shaped leathery leaves, 3in (8cm) long, are aromatic when bruised, and are commonly used dried in soups and stews. Excellent for shaping into a ball or a cone. Native to the Mediterranean region. Hardy to 10°F (-12°C), US zones 8–10.

PLANTING HELP   Plant in fertile, moist, well-drained soil in sun or partial shade. Propagate by cuttings in late summer. Water freely in hot weather and apply liquid feed every month from late spring to late summer. Prune and repot in spring if necessary; root pruning will restrict the growth of the tree. Protect from severe frost.

Bay with flowers

Box

Buxus sempervirens   A bushy, rounded, slow-growing evergreen tree that can grow to 15ft (4.5m) when planted in the ground but no more than 5ft (1.5m) in a container. The miniature varieties are smaller. The leaves are glossy and dark green, to 1¼in (3cm) long and are densely packed on to the branches. Boxes are excellent for topiary, easily trained to shape and have an unusual scent, especially after clipping. Hardy to 10°F (-12°C), US zones 8–10.

PLANTING HELP   Plant in fertile, well-drained compost in partial shade; if sited in full sun, make sure the soil is kept moist to avoid dull foliage and scorching. The container should be at least 10–12in (25–30cm) deep. Benefits from clipping twice every year, followed by fertilizing and mulching. Cuttings can be taken in summer or autumn and quite large pieces to 6in (15cm) long will often root.

Chamaecyparis

***Chamaecyparis lawsoniana* 'Green Pillar'**   One of the many cultivars of Lawson's cypress, which makes a narrow column of light green foliage. It is shown here clipped to form three spheres Hardy to 0°F (-18°C) US zones 7–10.

PLANTING HELP   Easy in any soil. Cuttings will root in summer. Clip regularly and a little at a time to keep the shoots green.

A bay tree in a Versailles pot at Het Loo

Clipped lawson's cypress with ivy and geraniums

Norfolk Island Pine

Araucaria heterophylla Norfolk Island Pine
An evergreen conifer that grows eventually up to
200ft (60m) but often used as a decorative plant in
large covered areas when young; suitable for
conservatory use for only a few years as it grows
quickly. Hardy to 32°F (0°C), US zone 10.

PLANTING HELP   Easily grown in any good
soil. Tolerant of salt winds, so useful near the sea.

Palm

Parlour Palm *Chamaedorea elegans*   An elegant,
slender-stemmed palm that grows 6–10ft (1.8–3m)
in the wild, but much less when grown in a
container. The terminal leaflets can be up to 2ft
(60cm) long, depending on the size of the plant.
Native to Mexico and Guatemala. These plants
can be grown in any zone but will be killed by the
first frost. Hardy to 32°F (0°C), US zone 10.

PLANTING HELP   Plant in fertile, rich, moist
but well-drained compost in shade or partial
shade. Water freely in growth. Replace the surface
compost or put in a bigger pot in spring.

Young Norfolk Island pines in slate pots in Dali

93

Index

INDEX

INDEX